The Term Structure
Of Interest Rates

The Intext Series in
MONETARY ECONOMICS

Consulting Editor
MICHAEL E. DE PRANO
Associate Professor of Economics
University of Southern California

THE TERM STRUCTURE OF INTEREST RATES

Financial Intermediaries and Debt Management

JACOB B. MICHAELSEN

University of California, Santa Cruz

Intext Educational Publishers
New York and London

For Hila, Aaron, and Rachel

Contents

Editor's Note

The increasing significance of monetary policy, and of monetary and fiscal influences on economic activity, indicates the importance of a clear understanding of these influences on the part of students, businessmen, and government authorities. The new insights into monetary and financial relationships which have developed in recent years can contribute greatly to this understanding if they are carefully integrated with the traditional analyses. Since many of the newer developments are presently comprehended only by the few specialists in any given area of research, a series of volumes by those directly involved in the various areas of money and finance was conceived.

Intext's Series in Monetary Economics was designed with these purposes in mind: first, to cover not only the subject of money and banking alone, but also the various other areas of economics in which monetary and financial influences are significant; second, to include even the most advanced levels of analysis in a way that is clear and meaningful to university-level students; and, third, to provide the instructor flexibility in courses and curricula dealing with the broader scope of monetary economics.

To accomplish this, a number of books will be offered, high in intellectual quality and analytical content. Although all material offered in the series will deal with the broad field of monetary economics, many of the volumes will investigate other areas of economics and are intended to provide the student stronger insights into the role of money and finance in other areas.

The volumes claim no one viewpoint and no one approach, except for analytical rigor. Institutional aspects are not avoided, but are not stressed. They are developed carefully where important for the analysis, and they do demonstrate that the traditional lines of demarcation between such emphases as institutional money and banking, financial institutions, money and capital markets, monetary policy, and international finance are becoming indistinguishable as research expands our knowledge of these areas.

Flexibility is achieved by presenting material in a series of volumes. This format provides expert coverage of individual subject areas and permits using different combinations of books to meet varying course objectives and requirements at both the undergraduate and graduate levels. The editor believes that the Intext Series in Monetary Economics makes a practical and effective contribution to greater understanding of monetary and financial influences in the economy.

MICHAEL E. DE PRANO

Preface

This book is intended for use in a variety of undergraduate courses in Money and Banking. I hope it will also be useful supplementary reading in courses on macroeconomics and on financial markets and institutions at both the undergraduate and beginning graduate level.

Students who have not yet taken intermediate macroeconomics may find it occasionally difficult; others who have done so will find it reasonably easy going. The former group will encounter most of their problems in the first three chapters, the first two of which set out the macroeconomic framework in which the problems that take up the rest of the book are cast.

Chapter 3 provides a framework within which to consider portfolio selection under uncertainty. These chapters are an adequate refresher in these matters for those who have already studied or are currently studying the material and may also serve as an adequate introduction for those who are encountering this analysis for the first time. Readers who are not fully familiar with either macroeconomics or portfolio selection may want to do some supplementary reading in standard texts on these subjects.

One further note: This volume attempts to give an objective account of what various economists think on the subject. In this respect it surveys the field. However, it also attempts to resolve some of the outstanding difficulties by offering a new approach to them. In this respect it aims at advancing the field. I hope that this attempt has not given too strong a partisan flavor to the exposition.

I am indebted to George J. Benston and Michael De Prano who read early drafts of this volume and provided both encouragement and valuable criticism. I am especially indebted to William T. Terrell who has been most helpful in suggesting improvement in the later stages of the writing. However, I have not taken all the advice which was so kindly offered. Because of this I must remain solely responsible for whatever errors and confusion remain.

The Term Structure
Of Interest Rates

Introduction

To the casual reader of the financial pages, yield quotations—price-earnings ratios and dividend yields for common stocks, yields to maturity for bonds—must appear as a bewildering welter of unrelated interest rates. Yet this seeming jumble of rates is not without order. The growing concern about interest rate structures and the empirical analysis which has accompanied it in recent years has not, however, produced a consensus about the process by which rate structures arise nor about the implications of these processes for the conduct of stabilization policy. Until quite recently textbooks confined themselves to discussing whether and how policy actions aimed at affecting the level of unemployment or the rate of inflation have their impact through the mediating role of "the interest rate." The principal objective of this book is to help rectify this situation by elucidating the process and factors that give rise to interest rate structures and exploring their implications for the conduct of policy.

One reason a common understanding in this area has not been achieved is the existence of certain conceptual difficulties connected with the notion of interest rate risk and with the idea of uncertainty generally. To increase the possibility of consensus it will be necessary to resolve these difficulties. I hope to achieve this by developing a conceptual model of interest rate determination under conditions of uncertainty that clearly establishes the theoretical character of the relationship between interest rate risk and term to maturity. In a word, I will argue that interest rate risk is a fundamental property of long-term capital commitments that increases as the durable life of the capital increases; that borrowers as well as lenders are averse to this risk; and that this aversion is reflected in premiums that make yields to maturity on dated securities larger than they would be if capital were perfectly mobile. Some argue that it is possible for shorter term securities to possess relatively more interest rate risk so

1

that these premiums could become negative. Such arguments have a very different conception of interest rate risk from the one advanced in this book. Moreover, the implications for managing the maturity composition of the government debt of these two positions differ considerably. For the former, in which the premiums stem from the immobility of capital, maturity composition and the magnitude of these premiums will be positively related; for the latter view, this relationship could be positive, negative or even nonexistent.

The book is divided into two major parts: the first (which includes the first three chapters) develops a theory of interest rate determination under uncertainty; the second (which includes the remaining chapters) reviews the work, empirical and theoretical, that bears on the rate structure problem and debt management policy. In Chapter 1, a model of interest rate determination under very simplified conditions is set forth. This model is of the long-run, stationary-state variety in which neither uncertainty nor the government sector have a role. Despite these shortcomings, the model does have special merit. It provides a way of illustrating the mechanics of the term structure of interest rates and a convenient way of classifying the various factors which influence the level and structure of interest rates.

In Chapter 2 we turn to a short-run income-expenditure model so that the impact of stabilizations policy on interest rates can be explored. Some important aspects of interest rate determination which can only be understood in the context of longer-term considerations will be brought to bear as the analysis proceeds. In Chapter 3 the problem of bringing uncertainty directly into account is confronted. Hopefully these three chapters will provide a firm basis for interpreting the empirical results and theoretical analysis that will be reviewed in the remainder of the book.

chapter 1

A Simple Classical Model of Interest Rate Determination

The models of aggregate economic behavior considered in this book are of the comparative static variety. Such models are particularly useful in analyzing the effects of variations in circumstances on both short- and long-run equilibrium at a point in time; however, they are essentially timeless. By excluding the passage of time these models make it extremely difficult to analyze the effects of uncertainty, for the essence of uncertainty, as I hope to make clear in Chapter 3, is the possibility of novelty; and change in this sense of the appearance of the new and different takes time. Theorists often use perfect competition as a point of reference to analyze market structure. However, in analyzing uncertainty, it is not appropriate to use perfect certainty as a point of reference in the same sense: uncertainty is not merely a departure from perfection.[1] Nevertheless, comparative static models can provide a useful point of departure in analyzing financial markets once their limitations regarding uncertainty are recognized.

In this chapter we will be concerned with time paths as well as equilibria both short- and long-run. Time paths in this context cannot strictly be regarded as equivalent to the passage of time since novelty is excluded. Nevertheless, certain dynamic considerations (dynamic meaning analysis of time paths as distinguished from the analysis of equilibria) will be introduced in a less than strict way for

[1] In Chapter 3 a major effort is made to confront what the recognition of uncertainty implies for interest rate determination. As I shall show in the later chapters, much effort has been expended avoiding such a confrontation. For a provocative discussion along these lines see Knight [34]. More than most, Knight was acutely aware of the difficulties the assumption of perfect certainty entailed. He emphasized on many occasions that choice can be given no meaning in a purely deterministic world.

two reasons. First, an understanding of the influence of the traditional factors of thrift and productivity on the level of the interest rate may be easier if the exposition is kept relatively simple. And second and more important, the alternative of developing a rigorous dynamic model would not only be exceedingly difficult but would overshadow one of the central concerns of this book which is to show the problematic character of comprehensive dynamic models under uncertainty.

A. INTEREST RATE DETERMINATION IN A TWO SECTOR ECONOMY

Let us begin with an economy composed of households and firms and incorporate a government sector later. To gain simplicity, assume that the size and demographic characteristics of the population, technology, and tastes remain constant over time. In addition, let us begin by assuming that the future is known with perfect certainty. To make clear how the maximizing effort of households and firms influence the long-run stationary-state equilibrium under these assumptions, it will be helpful to begin our analysis with a level of capital stock such that net saving and investment will be positive; that is, we enter the economy prior to its reaching a long-run equilibrium.

1. The Household Sector

Households receive income from the labor and capital services they provide to the production sector. The provision of these services requires labor and capital markets, but we shall consider here only the latter, assuming a competitive labor market with a straightforward determination of the wage rate.[2] The household decision which is crucial for our purposes is the allocation of income between present and future consumption because of its role in the determination of the level of the interest rate.

Let individual households experience life patterns of income such that their income from labor is more heavily concentrated in its earlier years. Assume also that households desire to maintain a fairly steady rate of consumption over their life time. To achieve this consumption pattern a household will save in its earlier years and

---

[2] The assumption means that we exclude the possibility of downward rigidity in wages and money illusion whereby labor supplied responds to nominal rather than real wage rates. The reason for doing so is to keep the focus sharply on the capital markets. Very little explicit attention will be given to the problems of wage determination, important as they are in their own right.

dissave in its later years. Given a population that is not changing in size, it is entirely possible for the saving of younger households to exactly offset the dissaving of the older ones thereby making net saving exactly zero. This situation corresponds, as will be seen more fully below, to the long-run stationary-state equilibrium in which the stock of capital which exists is exactly the size desired by firms in the production sector and the stock of financial claims to the return on this capital is exactly the size desired by households.

Since we are beginning this analysis at a point at which these stocks (which have a one to one correspondence) are smaller than they will be in the stationary state, it is necessary that net saving be positive at the outset. At such a point households will desire higher levels of consumption in the future than could be provided by saving just sufficient to even out lifetime consumption patterns. To achieve these higher levels households must defer greater amounts of current consumption than the evening out process would require. For individual households we assume that the higher the reward in terms of future consumption for each unit of current consumption deferred, the more current consumption will be deferred. This deferred current consumption takes the form of an increment to household wealth. It can be seen that a desired pattern of lifetime consumption can be translated into a lifetime pattern of saving or, alternatively, a lifetime of desired wealth. In this way the division between current consumption and saving depends on the level of wealth and, as we shall see shortly, the interest rate. This feature is the principal reason for designating this model classical.[3]

It will be helpful at this point to make more explicit the linkage between the capital stock held by firms, and savings, past and current, held by households. Firms may be viewed as producing perpetual income streams, the result of the difference between sales revenues and expenses, from the capital stock.[4] Claims to these streams take the form of perpetuities, financial assets which yield a fixed sum per period for the indefinite future. The supply of savings thus can also be viewed as the demand for perpetuities. Given the

---

[3] This version of the consumption and savings behavior is at variance with the one presented in the short-run macromodel in Chapter 2. Since we are not chiefly concerned with the particular form of the functional relationships involved in interest rate determination but rather with the general character of the process and how it is affected by uncertainty, this difference is of little significance.

[4] The use of money is implicit here. A discussion of the demand and supply of money in the context of this model appears in section C of this chapter. Further, since we are interested chiefly in interest rates, we will ignore product as well as labor markets. For purposes of calculating returns interest is not an expense.

promise of X units of return per period, and r the interest rate, the capital value of a claim is as follows: $V = X/r$.[5] Given the returns to the capital stock, there is, then, a unique relationship between the interest rate and the value of the capital stock, this value being also the value of household wealth. In what follows we shall view the savings process as the supplying of funds rather than the demanding of perpetuities.

This relationship between current consumption, wealth, and the interest rate is represented for the aggregate of households in Fig. 1-1. Given that individual households will save more, other

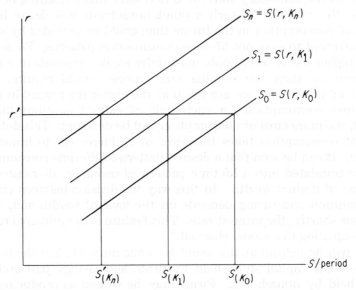

Fig. 1-1. Aggregate saving of the household for different levels of wealth or capital stock. r is the interest rate, S savings, and K the level of wealth or capital stock. $K_0 < K_1 < K_n$.

things equal, at higher interest rates, for a given level of the capital stock K_0 at time t_0, the amount of net saving will rise as the interest rate increases. Because the accumulation of savings over time increases the stock of wealth, the level of desired savings at a given level of the interest rate declines as the stationary state is approached. In Fig. 1-1, the capital stock at time t_0 is less than that at

---

[5] An example of the use of this notion of perpetuity is the dividend yield in which the annual dividend per share is divided by the market price per share. Implicit in this calculation is the empirical judgment that annual dividends and market value will remain constant in the future—which is what is assumed here—or that they will grow at the same rate in the future.

time t_1, K_1, and that is in turn less than that at time t_n, K_n. Correspondingly, at the given rate r', savings is less the greater the capital stock: $S'_{(K_n)} < S'_{(K_1)} < S'_{(K_0)}$. (Note: In labeling the figures in this book, subscripts in parenthesis have been attached to many variables. This notation indicates that the variable carrying the subscript takes the value mentioned in the subscript. For example, in Fig. 1-1, $S'_{(K_0)}$ indicates the value of savings at interest rate r', given the capital stock takes the value (K_0).)[6]

To keep the interest rate clearly at the center of our attention it will be helpful to state the relationship depicted in Fig. 1-1 (as well as in the figures which follow) in the following mathematical form:

(1-1) $r = f(K, S)$

By making the stock of capital and savings arguments of the function the interest rate is shifted to the left-hand side of the equation. This does not make the interest rate the dependent variable and the others the independent ones. Rather it serves to emphasize that we are more interested here in the interest rate structures than in the particular form of their functional relationship.

It will help to make the relationship between the savings schedules and the stock of capital clearer if we recognize that by assuming that the size and demographic character of the population to be fixed, we have assumed the stock of human wealth embodied in the labor force in the form productive knowledge and skills to be fixed. As a consequence, net investment can take place only in nonhuman capital. As the ratio of nonhuman to human wealth increases, additional increments to nonhuman wealth become less desirable. Put in more concrete terms, as the stock of nonhuman wealth owned by a household increases, increments in leisure become relatively more valuable. Given a fixed stock of human wealth, the accumulation of nonhuman wealth is subject to diminishing utility.

An alternative way to express this relationship is presented in Fig. 1-2. The horizontal axis represents the market value of the capital stock at a point in time. The positively sloped curves show the locus of points at which a given fraction of income would be saved. Given the labor force, a given capital stock K_0 makes possible an aggregate income $Y_{(K_0)}$. Saving $\alpha' Y_{(K_0)}$ out of this income at an interest rate $r'_{(K_0)}$ is greater than saving $\alpha Y_{(K_0)}$ at rate $r_{(K_0)}$ because as we have seen the quantity of desired saving is greater, other things equal, the higher the interest rate. Actual savings, of course, depend

---

[6] The system of notation used here is that developed by Laidler [35]. See footnote 3, Chapter 2.

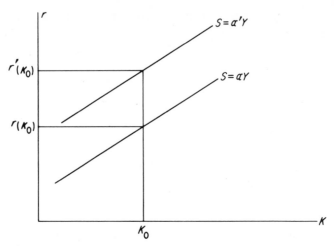

Fig. 1-2. The relationship between the capital stock and the interest rate at given levels of savings expressed as a fraction of aggregate income. K is the capital stock, Y is aggregate income, α is a fraction, $\alpha' > \alpha$.

on the opportunities to lend, and these are provided by the net investment made by the firm.

2. The Firm Sector

We assume, for convenience, that all firms are at less than optimal size and will all grow as capital accumulates. Thus, we may show the relationship between investment and the interest rate for both individual firms and the aggregate of all firms as in Fig. 1-3. For any given level of capital stock $K_0 < K_1 < K_n$ the amount of investment increases as the rate of interest declines. The reason for this is to be found in the law of variable proportions. As the amount of capital added at a given point in time prior to reaching long-run equilibrium to be combined with a given stock of labor increases, the productivity of capital diminishes. This is also why the amount of investment is less at a given interest rate the higher the level of the capital stock. Thus, as before $K_n > K_1 > K_0$ so that, given r', $I_{(K_n)} < I_{(K_1)} < I_{(K_0)}$. This relationship may be expressed as follows:

(1-2) $r = g(K, I)$

As with household saving behavior, the investment behavior of the firm can be depicted in stock as well as flow terms. The negatively sloped curves in Fig. 1-4 show the locus of points at which a given percentage of aggregate income would be invested. At capital stock K_0 and aggregate income $Y_{(K_0)}$, investment $\alpha' Y_{(K_0)}$ at rate

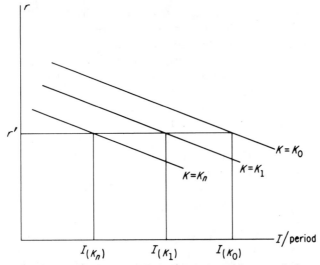

Fig. 1-3. The relationship between investment and the interest rate at given levels of the capital stock. I is investment, K_0 is capital stock and $K_0 < K_1 < K_n$.

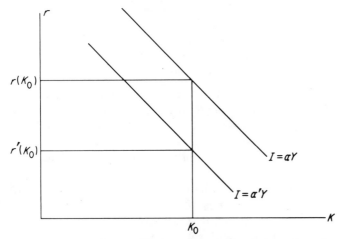

Fig. 1-4. The relationship between the capital stock and the interest rate at given levels of investment expressed as a fraction of aggregate income. K is capital stock, Y is aggregate income, α is a fraction, $\alpha' > \alpha$.

$r'_{(K_0)}$ is greater than investment $\alpha Y_{(K_0)}$ at rate $r_{(K_0)}$ because the quantity of desired investment is greater, other things equal, the lower the interest rate. As with saving in Fig. 1-2, actual investment depends on the opportunities to borrow, and these are provided by the saving of households.

Financial assets issued by firms and held by households link the capital stock to accumulated savings. Under the conditions of perfect certainty assumed here, the usual kinds of securities—common and preferred stocks, debentures, mortgage bonds, and the like—have no place since a principal feature of these assets is the uncertainty of their returns.[7] However, the representation of the relationship between the price of a perpetuity, its constant periodic return and the interest rate given above holds only in the special case in which the level of the interest rate is unchanging over time. Other things equal, the lower the price of a perpetuity, the more households are willing to hold; and the higher the price, the more firms wish to sell. In making that statement we are reporting what would happen if the level of the interest rate changed from a given single value in all future periods to a different, but constant, value in all future periods. We shall have occasion shortly to consider the case in which the interest rate may exhibit a pattern of variation over time. A more general formula for the price of a security which includes this case is as follows:

$$(1\text{-}3) \qquad\qquad V_0 = \sum_{t=1}^{\infty} \left[\frac{X_t}{(1 + r_t)^t} \right]$$

which reduces to $V_0 = X/r$ when r and K are constant for all t.[8]

3. Equilibrium, Short Run and Long Run

Having specified the factors that determine saving and investment behavior, two questions become apparent. (1) How are saving and investment equated given that the stock of capital is less than the equilibrium stock? And (2), how is the equilibrium stock of capital obtained? The interest rate is the equilibrating mechanism in both processes.

Consider first savings when the stock of capital is less than the equilibrium amount: that is, $K = K_0 < K_e$. Figure 1-5 depicts the short-run savings and investment equilibrium. The demand for investable funds, the investment schedule, and the supply of investable funds, the savings schedule, are such that at rate $r_{(K_0)}$, the market for investable funds is cleared and the fraction α of income is saved and invested.

Figure 1-6 depicts the short-run equilibrium in terms of the stock analysis. The curve denoted $\Sigma X_0 /r$ is the locus of market value of a

---

[7] We consider perpetuities with uncertain returns more fully in Chapter 3.

[8] Subscripts for interest rates will usually include only time designations as in Eq. 1-3 where r_t refers to the one-period rate to rule in period t. When it will help to make the discussion clearer, the notation $r_{(K_t)}$ will be used.

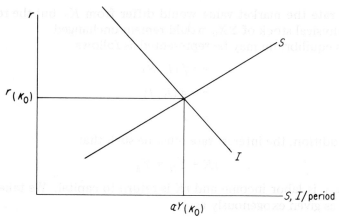

Fig. 1-5. Short-run equilibrium in the market for investable funds. $Y_{(K_0)}$ is aggregate income in period 0. Capital stock $K = K_0 < K_e$.

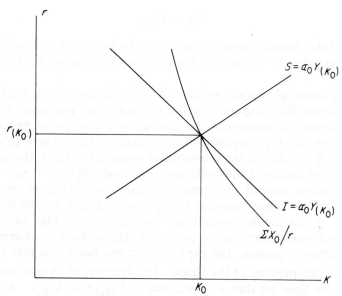

Fig. 1-6. The short-run equilibrium relationship between the interest rate and the stock capital given saving and investment are greater than zero. ΣX_0 is total returns to the capital stock.

given physical stock of capital. Recall from the perpetuity formula, $V = X/r$, when the returns are taken as given, V will vary only when r varies. To illustrate at the short-run equilibrium $K_0 = \Sigma X_0/r$. K_0 is market value only if the interest rate is r_0. $r = r_0$ here because, as depicted in Fig. 1-6, $S = I = \alpha_0 Y_{(K_0)}$ at r_0. Were $S = I$ at some other interest rate the market value would differ from K_0 but the returns to the physical stock of ΣX_0 would remain unchanged.

This equilibrium may be represented as follows:

(1-1) $$r = f(K, S)$$

(1-2) $$r = g(K, I)$$

(1-4) $$S = I$$

In addition, the interest rate must be such that

(1-5) $$rK + Y_H = Y_K$$

where Y_H is labor income and rK is return to capital. We take labor income as given exogenously as

(1-6) $$Y_H = Y_{(H_0)}$$

Finally,

(1-7) $$Y_K = Y_{(K_0)}$$

that is; total income must be such that the interest rate which establishes the value of capital stock also clears the market for investable funds.

This locus of market values $\Sigma X_0 / r$ holds only for a single time period when the long-run equilibrium state has not been reached. Under these circumstances the savings and investment process increases the stock of capital and consequently the returns to capital so that $\Sigma X > \Sigma X_0$. If the interest rate remains constant, the value of the stock of capital at the beginning of period will be $K = K_0 + \alpha Y_0$.[9]

Movement toward the stationary-state equilibrium in which the capital stock remains constant is depicted in Fig. 1-7. The left-hand portion of the figure reproduces the situation in Fig. 1-6. Since saving and investment exceed zero, the capital stock must grow over time. After n periods, the capital stock reaches K_n at rate $r_{(K_n)}$ as in the center portion of the figure. The fraction of income saved declines over time so that $\alpha_n < \alpha_0$ and $\alpha_n Y_{(K_n)} < \alpha_0 Y_{(K_0)}$. As noted above, the law of variable proportions insures that, other things equal, the lower the rate of return on it, the greater the existing stock of capital. Consequently, as long-run equilibrium is approached, the returns to incremental units of capital decline. Finally, in long-run equilibrium at t_e, the fraction of income saved and invested, α_e, becomes zero. The locus of points designated by $\Sigma X_e / r$ no longer rep-

[9] If the interest rate changes both K_0 and $\alpha_0 Y_0$ will be affected. Since perfect knowledge of the future is assumed, all such changes cause no special problem. Section B of this chapter deals with this situation.

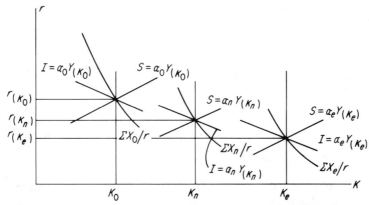

Fig. 1-7. The stationary-state equilibrium relationship between the interest rate and the stock of capital. At the equilibrium K_e, α_e is zero.

resents possible capital values at a single point in time but rather shows capital values at various interest rates that could persist without change indefinitely. At rate $r_{(K_e)}$ which will also persist indefinitely, the value of capital stock is K_e. The flow diagram corresponding to the right-hand portion of Fig. 1-7 is depicted in Fig. 1-8.[10]

This long-run equilibrium situation may be depicted by adding

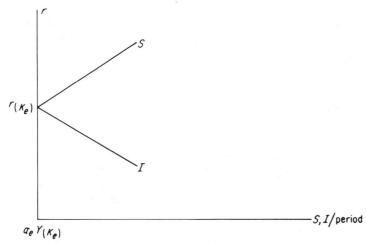

Fig. 1-8. Saving and investment schedules in the stationary-state equilibrium.

[10] Gross saving as well as gross investment will exceed zero in equilibrium but will be exactly offset by the dissaving of retired households and the maintenance of the capital stock.

the following equations to Eqs. 1-1 and 1-2:

(1-8) $S = 0$

(1-9) $I = 0$

(1-10) $Y_H = Y_{(H_e)}$

(1-11) $Y_{(K_e)} = Y_H + r_e K_e$

A declining time path for the short-run equilibrium interest rate, $r_{(K_0)} > r_{(K_n)} > r_{(K_e)}$, is depicted in Fig. 1-7. Should any significance be attributed to this pattern? The theories of household and enterprise behavior set out above contain nothing which entails a particular shape to the path by which the interest rate approaches its long-run equilibrium level. In an abstract model of this kind, declining, rising, or horizontal patterns are equally conceivable. Are there theoretical grounds for deciding whether successive savings and investment schedules shift equally or unequally as the capital stock grows? In addition to wealth and the interest rate, savings depends on the preferences of households similarly in addition to the capital stock and the interest rate, investment depends on technological possibilities. There is no a priori reason why preference and technology should be so balanced as to permit successive market clearing interest rates to be equal. If thrift dominates, rates will fall because greater levels of savings will be forthcoming at each interest rate so that markets will clear at successively lower interest rates; and similarly, if productivity diminishes, rates will rise. The pattern in Fig. 1-7, then, is but one of many possible ones that the approach to equilibrium might take.

B. THE TERM STRUCTURE OF INTEREST RATES IN THE STATIONARY STATE

It is worth exploring the implications of the alternative time paths of interest rates just sketched because this classical stationary-state model provides a useful point of departure for understanding the problems of risk and interest rate structures arising under conditions of uncertainty. This exploration will be particularly helpful in classifying the range of considerations that must be taken into account in analyzing models of forecasting time paths of interest rates. I shall argue that many of the current models are flawed by a failure to come to terms with some of these considerations.

Alternative time paths can be characterized by a structure of market yields to maturity on financial assets having different maturities, or more commonly by a term structure of interest rates. The notion of yield to maturity and its relationship to the interest rates used in the analysis so far will be made clear as we proceed. The problem before us now is to generate a term structure in the context of the classical model developed above.

Recall that the net saving which occurs prior to the stationary-state equilibrium is the result of gross saving by most households and dissaving by the older households. In long-run equilibrium the saving of younger units is just offset by the dissaving of the older units. Suppose that some households (those reaching retirement) begin to dissave at various times prior to reaching the long-run equilibrium capital stock. In view of the possibility of a changing level of the interest rate, we may ask what price these households can expect to receive for the perpetuities they sell and also what yields they received on their holdings over the period they held them.

A convenient way to answer these questions is to make use of specially designed perpetuities, fundamentally the same as the perpetual income streams defined above but which simplify the mechanics of constructing a term structure in this model. Consider a perpetuity which pays X units at the end of each period beginning with a period in which the equilibrium stock of capital is reached, but which pays nothing prior to that time.[11] The price of this discounted perpetuity at the beginning of a period e is[12]

$$(1\text{-}12) \qquad V_{(K_e)} = \frac{X}{r_{(K_e)}}$$

Given that the special perpetuity must reach a price of $V_{(K_e)}$ at t_e, what value will it have prior to that time when no periodic payments accrue to its holder?

The value will be, three periods prior to equilibrium, following the example used below in Fig. 1-9:

$$(1\text{-}13) \qquad V_{(K_0)} = \frac{V_{(K_e)}}{(1 + r_{(K_0)})(1 + r_{(K_1)})(1 + r_{(K_2)})}$$

which is equivalent to $V_{(K_e)}/(1 + r_{(K_e)})^3$ in the special case $r_{(K_0)} =$

---

[11] Treating a perpetuity as a discounted note prior to reaching the stationary state simplifies the problems of exposition. Thus, it is possible to draw Fig. 1-9 without being concerned about the "coupons" or periodic payments. These payments would require saw-tooth paths as the value of the perpetuity would fall by the amount of the payment just after the coupon was "clipped." Nothing of significance is lost by this simplification.

[12] To illustrate, if X be 50 units or dollars and $r_{(K_e)}$ be 5 percent, then $V_{(K_e)}$ will be 1,000 dollars.

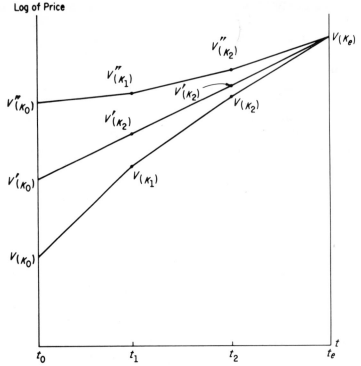

Fig. 1-9. The time path of the price of a discounted perpetuity under three different time paths of the interest rate.

$r_{(K_1)} = r_{(K_2)} = r_{(K_e)}$.[13] It is especially important to note that the interest rates used here are one-period rates; that is, the rate that clears the market for savings and investment at the corresponding level of

[13] Assuming a rate of 5 percent in this special case and the figures in footnote 12, we have

$$V'_{(K_0)} = \frac{\$1,000}{(1.05)^3} = \$863.84$$

For a declining time path

$$V_{(K_0)} = \frac{\$1,000}{(1.07)(1.06)(1.05)} = \$838.71$$

For a rising time path

$$V''_{(K_0)} = \frac{\$1,000}{(1.03)(1.04)(1.05)} = \$883.55$$

The mechanics involved are treated more fully below. Had there been payments prior to equilibrium, $V_{(K_0)}$ would have been $1,000 in the first instance, less than $1,000 for a declining time path, and greater than $1,000 for a rising time path.

the capital stock in each successive period, just as rate $r_{(K_0)}$ does in Fig. 1-5. The numerator in Eq. 1-13 can be derived so simply because, after equilibrium, successive one-period rates do not change.

Figure 1-9 shows three possible time paths of value for a discounted security as the stationary state is approached. The vertical axis represents the logarithm of value and the horizontal axis represents time—in this instance we consider the three periods prior to reaching the stationary state.[14]   Line $V_{(K_0)}$, $V_{(K_e)}$ corresponds to the declining pattern of rates depicted in Fig. 1-7. The slopes $V_{(K_1)}/V_{(K_0)} = 1 + r_{(K_0)}$, $V_{(K_2)}/V_{(K_1)} = 1 + r_{(K_1)}$ and $V_{(K_e)}/V_{(K_2)} = 1 + r_{(K_2)}$. Thus, the consequence of a successive decline in the one-period rate together with the absence of periodic payments in the initial three periods, produces a time path of price which rises less steeply in each successive period.   Once the stationary state is reached, the time path depends on the way in which payments are made.   For example, if a single payment is made at the end of each period, the price will rise from $V_{(K_e)}$ just after payment is made.[15] Line $V'_{(K_0)}$, $V_{(K_e)}$ represents constancy in one-period rates and line $V''_{(K_0)} V_{(K_e)}$ represents a rising trend in them.

We now can give an account of the yields to maturity of which the term structure of interest rates is composed using as our basis the notion of a time pattern of successive one-period rates. We may begin by asking what yield would a household receive if it held a discounted perpetuity for a finite period, say from t_0 to t_e in Fig. 1-9. As before, the yield is a function of the growth in value of the discounted perpetuity, in this instance $V_{(K_e)}/V_{(K_0)}$. It will be helpful to adopt a notation that will distinguish among the various interest rates and yields under consideration. Let R denote a yield on a holding over n periods beginning at time t. In the present example, $R_{3,0}$ is the yield on the discounted perpetuity from t_0 to t_e expressed as the average one-period rate that will be realized over these three periods. Let $r_{n,t,s}$ be an n period interest rate to rule beginning at time s as seen at time t. Thus $r_{1,0,2}$ is the one-period rate to rule in period 2 as seen at t_0, the $r_{(K_2)}$ described just above. Then $V_{(K_e)}/V_{(K_0)} = (1 + R_{3,0})^3$.

Moreover, since

$$V_{(K_e)}/V_{(K_0)} = [(V_{(K_1)}/V_{(K_0)})(V_{(K_2)}/V_{(K_1)})(V_{(K_e)}/V_{(K_2)})],$$

[14] The use of a logarithmic scale in the value dimension makes it possible to depict one-period rates as straight lines. Exponential curves would be required if the vertical scale was arithmetical.

[15] See footnote 11 for an account of this saw-tooth pattern.

(1-14) $(1 + R_{3,0})^3 = (1 + r_{1,0,0})(1 + r_{1,0,1})(1 + r_{1,0,2})$

Similarly, the yield on a holding from t_0 to t_2 would be $(1 + R_{2,0})^2 = (1 + r_{1,0,0})(1 + r_{1,0,1})$. For a single period, $1 + R_{1,1} = 1 + r_{1,0,0}$. Since $r_{1,0,2} < r_{1,0,1} < r_{1,0,0}$, $R_{3,0} < R_{2,0} < R_{1,0}$. A schedule or structure of these yields over differing holding periods would therefore show a negatively sloping relationship between yields and the time period involved. This situation is depicted in Fig. 1-10 by the upper curve. It is important to note that the yields just described are not strictly yields to maturity since the securities in question are perpetuities. For the moment let us assume that the holders convert the securities to cash at the end of the corresponding holding periods so that the securities "mature" for some households. We shall return to this matter shortly.

Returning then to Fig. 1-9, the situation depicted by line $V'_{(K_o)}V_{(K_e)}$ is one in which the successive one-period rates remain constant. Consequently, not only is $R'_{3,0}$ the geometric average of the three one-period rates $r'_{1,0,0}$, $r'_{1,0,1}$, $r'_{1,0,2}$ but is equal to them. In Fig. 1-10 this relationship produces the horizontal term structure. Similarly, line $V''_{(K_o)}V_{(K_e)}$ in Fig. 1-9 depicts the situation of a rising trend in one-period rates and corresponds to the lower curve in Fig. 1-10.

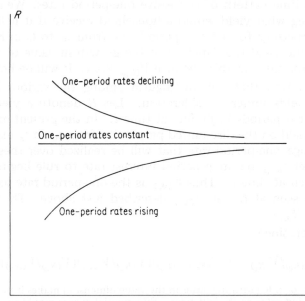

Fig. 1-10. Term structure of yields to maturity corresponding to the three time paths of price displayed in Fig. 1-9 as seen at t_0. R is yield to maturity, M is term to maturity.

In developing this account of the term structure, we have assumed that all households and firms have perfect knowledge of the supply and demand functions which determine successive one-period rates.[16] In addition, transactions were assumed to be costless. Under these assumptions prices cannot deviate from the time path implied by the sequence of a time-period rise. Because the prices of securities are known with certainty, it does not matter whether yields to maturity are defined in terms holding horizons or in terms of the life of the security in question since the return realized over the holding period does not depend on the life of the security. In other words, the $R_{n,t}$ will always turn out, no matter what the term to maturity, to have been correct in retrospect at time $t + n$. Later, when these assumptions are dropped, the fact that actual securities have finite lives that may differ from holding horizons will become important and we will make a sharp distinction between holding periods and terms to maturity.

Further, whatever the shape of the term structure prior to reaching the stationary-state equilibrium, in equilibrium it will be horizontal initially and remain so over time since the one-period rates remain so over time since the one-period rates remain constant. The converse of this is that a term structure which is not horizontal is evidence in this model that the long-run stationary-state equilibrium level of the capital stock has not been reached. We shall have occasion to recall this aspect of yield curves below.

However, before we go further, we should consider what the implication of this analysis is for, say, the observed structure of yields to maturity on U.S. Government bills and bonds. Do the yield curves observed in the daily press reflect the course of one-period interest rates expected to rule in the future? Are there other factors beyond those incorporated in the models of household and firm behavior described above that have an influence? There is no consensus about the answers to these questions and much more will be said about the matter below. For the moment, it is important to note that in the world where term structures can be observed, other things do not remain constant. However, we need, but do not have, validated theories of the way many of these other things behave. For example, we do not know much about the determinants of population growth, of technological change, and of changes in taste and other variables, but we do know that all these variables do change and these changes affect interest rates. Consequently we do not

---

[16] Certainty means that perfect knowledge of the real variables that determine successive supply and demand schedules for loanable funds, and hence successive one-period rates, is available at no cost. In the absence of perfect certainty forecasting is not a costless process. The problems entained by a costly forecasting process are taken up in Chapter 3.

know whether or when the long-run equilibrium might be reached. In addition, it is difficult to tell whether changes in security prices reflect movements toward equilibrium as in Fig. 1-9 or changes in the variables which determine equilibrium and, hence, in the point of equilibrium itself. Given this state of incomplete knowledge, little basis exists for completely confident statements about the significance of the observed behavior of term structures for stabilization policies.

It is sometimes possible to simplify a complex reality successfully by focusing a few important variables as, for example, in studies of the supply and demand for agricultural products. Thus, one hesitates to argue that the situation is too complex to make easy use of the notion that the term structure reflects the future course of one-period rates. Yet it must be so argued. The interest rate, or better, interest rates, are central prices in a market economy. They play significant roles in a wide range of markets. The ways in which interest rates influence and are influenced by this wide range of consumption and investment decisions are not well understood but are nonetheless important for understanding how securities markets work and what their workings imply for stabilization policy.

We shall keep complexities and uncertainties at the center of the analysis which follows, where they become key features in the notion of interest rate risk. For the moment we note the kinds of real variables about which knowledge is necessary to predict the course of one-period interest rates. We need information on savings behavior of households, on investment opportunities open to firms, on factors influencing growth in population and changes in its demographic characteristics, on factors influencing technological change and on factors influencing tastes for consumption goods. Let us now turn to a consideration of the government sector as a first step in gaining an understanding of policy variables which bear on the level and structure of interest rates.

C. THE GOVERNMENT SECTOR AND MONEY IN THE STATIONARY STATE

So far neither money nor financial institutions have been considered explicitly[17] nor has provision been made for government expenditure and taxation. Monetary and fiscal policy action do influence

---

[17]How the transactions in discounted perpetuities by retiring households just described were facilitated was not made explicit. Presumably, these are costless. In a world of perfect certainty they could be made in kind without the need for money. This point is taken up below.

the level and structure of interest rates. Because one of our principal aims is to examine the implications of the workings of the private financial sector for stabilization policy, explicit consideration of monetary and fiscal institutions is essential. As a first step, supply and demand for money functions will be included in the stationary-state model outlined above. After establishing the character of the relationship between the interest rate and money in the stationary-state equilibrium in the remainder of this chapter, we will go on in Chapter 2 to develop a framework for dealing with shorter-run policy questions such as inflation and unemployment. The focus will be on how policy can be used to influence the level and structure of rates and thereby affect the behavior of firms and households. No attempt will be made here to review in detail the controversies about the proper specification of macroeconomic models and the implications of alternative formulations for the conduct of policy.

One way to show what the impact of money is on the interest rate in the stationary-state equilibrium is to continue the model as developed so far by adding equations for the supply of and demand for money. The first step is to bring money and the price level explicitly into the system. To do this, money supply and demand functions are required. For the moment, let the money supply function be

$$(1\text{-}15) \qquad\qquad M_s = M^*$$

where the nominal money stock is arbitrarily determined by the monetary authority. Much more than the mechanical linkage between the monetary stock and the monetary base controlled by the monetary authorities suggested here is necessary for a fully satisfactory understanding of policy questions.[18] We shall return to some of these complexities later.

The demand for money may be expressed as

$$(1\text{-}16) \qquad\qquad \frac{M_d}{P} = h\left(r, \frac{K}{P}\right)$$

where M_d is the nominal money stock, P the price level and K the capital stock. Thus, M_d/P is the real value of the money. We assume that households and firms are aware of the price level and are consequently not susceptible to illusions about the purchasing power of money holdings. While the monetary authority determines the nominal money stock, the desire of households and firms for holding

---

[18] For a full treatment of the supply of money see De Prano [15].

purchasing power determine the real money stock as given by the arguments in function h.[19]

With respect to these arguments, assume that the real balances demanded vary inversely with the interest rate and directly with the real value of the capital stock. This formulation is formally comparable to the conventional Keynesian demand for money function comprising a speculative component related to the level of the interest rate and a transaction component related to the level of income. Recall that $Y_K = rK + Y_H$ so that here the size of the capital stock may be regarded as a satisfactory indicator of, or proxy for, the level transactions. But not too much should be made of this resemblance, Equation 1-16 is an equation of convenience, a full justification for its character being beyond the scope of this book. However, a word or two about positing a demand for money under the conditions of certainty assumed in the stationary-state equilibrium may help to indicate some of the problems involved. As will be argued later, the Keynesian speculative demand for money cannot be sustained in the stationary-state equilibrium. Thus, the rationale for the relationship between real balances and the interest rate is called into question. Moreover, the rationale for a transaction demand for money under certainty is far from clear. In the stationary-state equilibrium no changes of any kind can occur. Consequently, the pattern of all transactions would be known once and for all with the result that transactions could be arranged without the use of money. If some uncertainty be admitted to justify the need for money, we begin to move away from the notion of a stationary state. As we shall see, the need for some kind of uncertainty to make a transaction demand believable has implications for understanding the character of interest rate risk and its impact on the term structure.[20]

Given the equations defining equilibrium without money and Eqs. 1-15 and 1-16 we need add only

(1-17) $$M_s = M_d$$

to reach a stationary-state equilibrium, subject to the caveat just mentioned concerning uncertainty. This solution is depicted in Fig. 1-11. Schedule $I'I'$ represents the locus of points at which investment in real capital by firms is zero and corresponds to the schedule $I = \alpha_e Y_{(K_e)}$ in Fig. 1-7. Schedule II represents the locus of points at which the capital stock and real money holdings of firms are just suf-

---

[19] For a full treatment of the demand for money see Laidler [35].

[20] For an interesting recent discussion that relates the demand for transaction and with an explicit treatment of the cost of information see Brunner and Meltzer [7]. Their discussion makes clear the unsettled state of the theory of the demand for money.

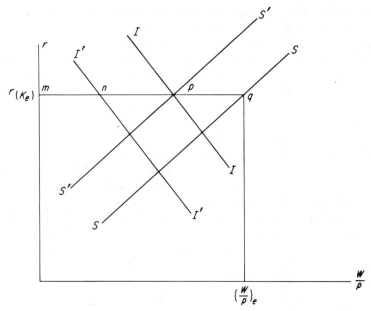

Fig. 1-11. The demand for money in the stationary-state equilibrium. W is wealth which includes both the capital stock and real
money balances, and P is the price level.

ficient to keep the number of outstanding perpetuities constant and
net investment zero. Schedule $S'S'$ represents the locus of points at
which holdings of perpetuities by households is zero and corresponds
to the schedule $S = \alpha_e Y_{(K_e)}$ in Fig. 1-7. Schedule SS represents the
locus of points at which the holdings of perpetuities and real cash
balances by households remain unchanged.

Note that the equilibrium interest rate $r_{(K_e)}$ is given by the intersection of the II and $S'S'$ schedules at p. In the absence of money
(or better, where money is not explicitly considered) the equilibrium
interest rate would be given by the intersection of the $I'I'$ and $S'S'$
schedules. The explicit introduction of money here implies that the
real balances held by firms, the amount given by np on the line extending from $r_{(K_e)}$ to the right, together with the capital stock, the
amount given by mn on the same line, yield the equilibrium rate
$r_{(K_e)}$ on the margin. Line segment pq measures real cash balances
and segment mp, the value of perpetuities held by households. Following the reasoning just applied to cash holdings of firms, cash
holdings of households yield implicitly the equilibrium rate of interest on the margin.

Thus, money is productive wealth for both firms and households in this model, though the rationales advanced for money as a factor of production and as a facilitator of transactions stand chiefly as devices of convenience. Whatever the appropriate theory of the demand for money may be, the real value of the money stock depends not on its quantity, but rather on its existence. The same is not true of the capital stock, the value of which depends in a fundamental way on its physical properties. Given the same nominal money stock, and different demand and supply schedules for real capital apart from money—that is, different $I'I'$ and $S'S'$ schedules—the demand and supply schedule for real capital plus real balances—the II and SS schedules would also be different. How they would differ would, of course, depend on behavioral questions we have skirted here by use of the rationales for money holding just described. However, since the demand and supply schedules for real capital play a fundamental role in determining the interest rate in this model, they must also play a significant role in determining the demand for money. This is expressed by the interest rate and capital stock arguments in the demand for money equation 1-16.

The implications of explicit introduction of money for the term structure are minor. As we have seen, the equilibrium levels of the interest rate may well differ because of the existence of money though not because of its nominal quantity. Taking this impact on the level into account only changes the location of the term structure at a point in time as by displacement of the yields in Fig. 1-10 upward, but does not change the interpretation that, in this model, the yield reflects the future course of one-period rates.

As for stabilization problems, there is no need for a monetary authority once the nominal money is in existence because the price level P automatically adjusts to insure that real balances supplied are equal to real balances demanded. We skip over here the problems of how the price level behaves, given a fixed nominal money stock, as equilibrium is approached. Very briefly, P must decline as output increases.[21] Once the stationary state is reached, and even before, there is no need for a monetary authority since there are no stabilization problems.

Once we recognize that the economy may not be in long-run equilibrium we must also recognize that it can be in short-run disequilibrium. Since we are concerned here with the conduct of stabilization policy we need to expand our analytical apparatus so that the impact of government fiscal and monetary policy actions on un-

---

[21] A declining price level under the conditions assumed here—certainty, flexible wage rates and the absence of money illusion—will not produce unemployment.

employment and inflation[22] are taken into account. Our concern here, however, will be less with the way policy actions finally affect price and economic activity and more with their impact on the level and structure of interest rates both in the short term and in the long.

---

[22] Thus, if inflation is unanticipated it will lead to short-run disequilibrium as its impact becomes apparent. Thus, some of the assumptions made here (see footnote 20) must be modified if stabilization policy has a place in the analysis.

A Model of Stabilization Policy
and Interest Rate Determination

With the help of the classical model set out above we were able to identify the nonpolicy variables that played a significant role in the determination of the interest rate. In this chapter we seek to identify the policy variables which influence the interest rate and gain some understanding of how they work. To do this we shall employ the income-expenditure approach used to deal with short-run stabilization questions. We will keep to a fairly simple version of the macroeconomic model commonly used for these purposes, focusing first on its behavior under conditions of unemployment and then examining its behavior under inflation.

Assume in this economy that there are sufficient resources to meet any level of aggregate demand likely to arise so that increases in aggregate demand can be met by increases in output without producing pressures which cause prices to rise. Thus, we begin in a situation of unemployment and ask what happens to the level of the interest rate as efforts are made by the authorities to reach full employment. We assume here, in addition, that the capital stock is below its long-run equilibrium level so that both savings and investments can exceed zero. This assumption is usually implicit in short-run analyses.

As before, there are three sectors in the economy: the householder which consumes and saves, the firm sector which invests and generates returns, and the government sector which now does much more than create an initial money stock. The government sector now makes expenditures, levies taxes and manipulates the money stock. In addition to this much expanded role of government, the behavior of the household sector will differ slightly from the pattern established in the classical model. While this change is not of great moment, it will be helpful to provide some reason for it.

The behavior of consumption expenditures in the classical model depends on the capital stock and the interest rate, since savings, which is explicitly treated in figures and equations of Chapter 1, is simply income minus consumption. Thus, at a given level of the interest rate, consumption increases as the capital stock grows and for a given level of the capital stock, increases as the interest rate declines. In the income-expenditure approach, consumption expenditures are made to depend on income alone.

How can the discrepancies between the two models be resolved for our purposes here? With respect to the omission of the influence of the interest rate on consumption and hence on savings, we may note that in more complex macroeconomic models of this kind, the influence of the interest rate is not omitted. If we keep in mind that it is possible to incorporate the interest rate as a factor influencing household behavior at the cost of increasing the complexity of the exposition, little will be lost if we keep to the simpler model.

Whether consumption is made to depend on income rather than the capital stock or wealth poses no special problem either. In the income-expenditure approach, income is a proxy for the wealth which remains implicit. In the classical model, as given by Eq. 1-5, income and wealth are tied together directly by means of the interest rate: wealth, a stock, is the capitalized value of income, a flow.[1] Since the income-expenditure approach is concerned with flows, and especially with how to alter them in the short run, the focus on income is understandable. Because of this exclusive focus on the short run, the income-expenditure approach obscures the long-run considerations that bear on the term structure of interest rates. As a result, the term structure has not been satisfactorily incorporated in such models. I shall not attempt to give explicit recognition to these long-run considerations in the context of this approach but shall rely instead on the discussion of them presented in Chapter 1 to provide the necessary background qualifications.

Let consumption then be the usual increasing function of current disposable income such that on the average over the range of income at issue and at the margin households will save some fraction of their disposable income. We will take this to mean not that the capital stock has no influence on consumption behavior but rather that the capital stock has not yet reached its stationary-state equilibrium

---

[1] A further complication affecting the relationship between income and wealth is that, when the economy is at less than full employment, the income is less than would be calculated by applying the interest rate to the stock of wealth as in Eq. 1-5. Moreover, this equation implies an unchanging interest rate. We will ignore these complications here.

level.[2]   Investment is a declining function of the interest rate, the influence of the capital stock remaining implicit as with consumption
and savings behavior.   Government expenditures are taken to be
exogenous, being determined in ways which do not depend on real
variables in the system, at least not in the sense in which they enter
the maximization process of households and firms, but which may
have important effects on these variables.

The model is in equilibrium when the aggregation of these three
classes of expenditures, as determined by these functions, is equal to
the level of income.   The model is set out in Fig. 2-1.[3]   Panel (a)

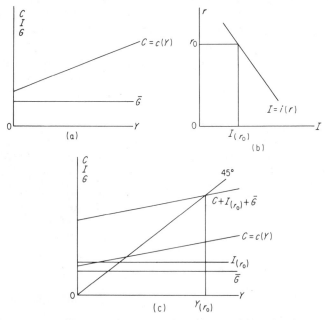

Fig. 2-1. The simple geometry of income determination.
C is consumption, I investment, G government expenditure, Y income, and r the rate of interest. c and i denote
functional relationships, while the bar over G indicates
that it is an exogenous variable.

[2] In the stationary-state equilibrium net saving is zero; consequently, the
marginal propensity to consume must become unity.   A consumption function
of the kind depicted in Fig. 2-1(a) is not consistent with requirement since its
slope is constant and less than unity.   We shall assume that the stationary state is
sufficiently far off that we can ignore the problem such a linear consumption
function poses.

[3] The income expenditure model presented here draws heavily from the one
Laidler developed [35].   This was convenient for me because he did his job so
well but it will also be convenient for the reader who wishes to use Laidler's
volume in conjunction with this one.

shows the consumption function $C = c(Y)$ and the exogenous level of government expenditure $\overline{G}$. Panel (b) shows the investment function $I = i(r)$ which is similar to the investment relationship depicted above in Fig. 1-3. The quantity of investment undertaken can be determined if the level of the interest rate is known. For the moment we may assume it to be r_0 so that investment is I_0. This level of investment can be added to consumption and government expenditures as shown in panel (c) to produce the $C + I_0 + \overline{G}$ curve. The 45° line is the locus of all points at which expenditure, measured on the vertical axis, can be equal to income, measured on the horizontal axis. The aggregate expenditure curve cuts the 45° line at only one point corresponding to income of Y_0. At this point the expenditures given by the functional relationships can be supported by the available income; that is, the system is in an equilibrium position at a level of income Y.

Should the interest rate take on a value different from r_0, the level of investment and hence of equilibrium level of income would change. It remains to be shown how the interest rate is determined in this model. Nevertheless, there is implicit in Fig. 2-1 a relationship between the equilibrium levels of income and the level of interest rate. Once this is made explicit it will be easy to see how the interest rate is determined in the model.

Panel (a) in Fig. 2-2 shows the relationship between investment and the rate of interest. Panel (b) shows various relationships between aggregate expenditure and income, all based on the same consumption function and level of government expenditure, when the interest rate takes on various values: $r_0 > r_1 > r_2$. The lower the rate of interest the higher the level of investment and hence the higher the level of aggregate expenditure as shown in panel (b). In this panel $C + I_{(r_2)} + G$ lies above $C + I_{(r_1)} + G$ and the latter, in turn, lies above $C + I_{(r_0)} + G$. Corresponding to each of these aggregate expenditure curves are the equilibrium levels of income, $Y_{(r_2)} > Y_{(r_1)} > Y_{(r_0)}$. The lower the level of the interest rate the higher is this level of income and the interest rate is plotted as the curve IS in panel (c).[4]

To complete the model it is necessary to provide a mechanism to arrive at a single interest rate from among the range of rate consistent with the IS function depicted in panel (c) of Fig. 2-2. In the classical model this interest rate was achieved by the clearing of the market

---

[4] IS refers to the fact that in a model without government expenditure any point along this curve would be one at which investment was equal to saving. It is now general practice to use this label for any curve showing real-goods market equilibrium.

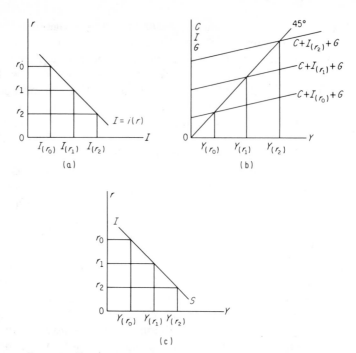

Fig. 2-2. The equilibrium relationship between the rate of interest and the level of income implicit in the model of real-goods market.

for loanable funds subject to the influence of the stock of capital. Recall that, as shown in Fig. 1-6, the interest rate was such as to make the price of new perpetuities issued to finance investment expenditures equal to the price on the outstanding stock of perpetuities. In the present income-expenditure model, savings does not respond to the interest rate and the stock of wealth is not an explicit variable. Consequently, we must turn to an alternative mechanism for interest rate determination.

The way the interest rate is made determinate in this simple income-expenditure model is by giving the demand for money a pivotal role. Recall that in the classical model, productivity and thrift were sufficient to produce an equilibrium interest rate The introduction of money altered the final equilibrium but was not essential to achieving it.[5] The demand for money enters here in a fundamentally different way so that we must add monetary or "non-

---

[5] See Chapter 1, page 24. In the classical model equilibrium could be achieved without money whereas money is an essential element in the determination of the interest rate and thus of equilibrium.

real" variables to the list of real variables that influence the level of the interest rate.

We may take the money demand equation 1-16, $M_d/P = h(r, K/P)$, as representing the demand for money here but modifying it to reflect the use of income instead of the stock of capital as a key factor in keeping with the emphasis on short-run flows in the income-expenditure model. Thus we have

$$(2\text{-}1) \qquad \frac{M_d}{P} = j\left(r, \frac{Y}{P}\right)$$

As before, households and firms desire smaller real balances the higher the interest rate, and larger real balances the higher the level of real income. The influence of the interest rate on the portfolio decisions of households and firms will be discussed more fully in later chapters. Suffice it that very little can be said about it without in some way introducing uncertainty.[6]

This formulation is equivalent to asserting that the demand for money measured in units of constant purchasing does not vary with the price level. A word of caution about price level variations may be useful at this point. First, to make the assertion that the price level does not matter does not mean that a changing price level does not matter. The latter involves inflation or deflation and can matter very much. For the moment we have taken the price level as given. However, when we do this we implicitly make the nominal interest rate identical to the real interest rate, the former being defined as the relation of the current price of a perpetuity to future nominal money payments unadjusted for price level changes, the latter being defined as the relation of current price of a perpetuity to future money payments expressed in the same real terms as the current price. If the price level is expected to change, that is, if inflation or deflation is expected, nominal and real interest rates will diverge.[7] We will have occasion to consider the effects of divergences below.

As in the classical model, we assume as a first approximation that the supply of money is completely under the control of the monetary authorities, taking their behavior as determined by considerations exogenous to or outside the model. Given both supply and demand

---

[6] The same is true, as we have seen in Chapter 1, for rationalizing a transaction demand for money. See page 22.

[7] Under the assumption of certainty which we have not yet abandoned, nominal rates will reflect the fact that nominal receipts in future periods will be greater (smaller) under inflation (deflation) than they would be if the price levels were constant. Nominal rates are derived from nominal values, real rates from nominal values adjusted for purchasing power changes.

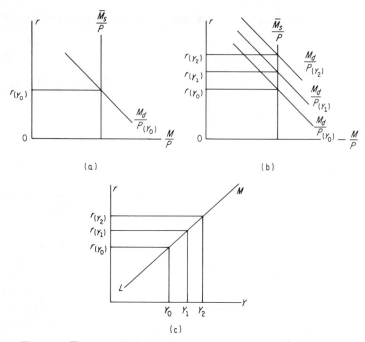

Fig. 2-3. The equilibrium relationship between the rate of interest and the level of income implicit in the model of the money market. M is the quantity of money and P the price level so that M/P is the quantity of money measured in units of constant purchasing power. The subscripts s and d stand for supplied and demanded and the bar over M_s indicates that it is an exogenous variable.

functions for money we can then see how the achievement of equilibrium in the money market is instrumental to reaching an equilibrium level of income.

Equilibrium in the money market is depicted in Fig. 2-3. Panel (a) shows the relation of real balance demanded and the interest rate at a given level of income Y_0. With a given supply of money $\overline{M}_s$ and price level P this market would be in equilibrium at the interest rate $r_{(Y_0)}$. As before, with the market for current flows of goods and services, we can specify one variable, the interest rate, only if we specify another variable, the level of income. In panel (b) the effect of different levels of income on the equilibrium level of the interest is shown. As was just argued, the demand for money at any interest rate increases as income rises; the curve relating the demand for money to the interest rate must shift to the right as income rises. Thus $Y_2 > Y_1 > Y_0$. Given M_s and P, higher levels of income produce higher equilibrium interest rates. This positive relationship between income and the interest rate is graphed in panel (c) and is labeled, as is customary, *LM*.

We are now in a position to complete the model by showing how a single interest rate and level of income are achieved. We have two different equilibrium relationships between the interest rate and income. The *IS* curve shows conditions required for expenditures and income to be in equilibrium. The *LM* curve shows the conditions required for nonmonetary and monetary wealth to be just held, given the price level. Since expenditure and money-holding decisions are made by the same decision units, we can join these two conditions as in Fig. 2-4. The equilibrium income Y_e and interest rate r_e are the only two values of these variables which make possible a mutually consistent set of expenditure and money-holding decisions.

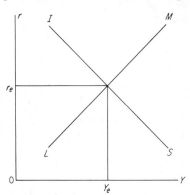

Fig. 2-4. The determination in the complete model of the equilibrium levels of the interest rate and of income.

While this model is well-adapted to analyzing short-run stabilization problems, it is not without its shortcomings for understanding the term structure of interest rates. Thus, the model does not specify the time dimension to be assigned to r_e in Fig. 2-4. One answer, and presumably the most appropriate, is that it is a one-period rate corresponding to the span of time by which income in the horizontal axis is measured. Even though this produces no problem in the context of this approach, the notion of a single interest rate spanning an indeterminate period of time provides no basis for considering the structure of interest rates spanning differing periods of time.

This difficulty tends to be obscured by the way money and wealth are treated. Implicit in the inverse relationship of the interest to the demand for money is a direct relationship between the interest and the demand for perpetuities. In many discussions of the model the perpetuities are taken to be bonds, often only of government issue, of indeterminate length. By leaving the demand for wealth implicit and focusing sharply on the demand for money, the problem of term to maturity becomes submerged. The virtue of the classical model is that it makes the need for specifying the time pattern of short-period rates explicit and suggests the factors which should be considered in developing a theory of this pattern. Once this shortcoming is recognized, appropriate steps can be taken to keep the short-run character of this income expenditure from obscuring the term structure question.

One of the important features of this income-expenditure model is that it lends itself readily to analyzing the impact of changes in policy and other variables. Underlying the IS curve in Fig. 2-4 are given consumption and investment functions as well as a given level of government expenditure and taxes. A given demand for money function, a given supply of money and given price level lie behind the LM curve. Let us look at the way the model responds to changes in these underlying factors.

A change in any of the factors underlying the IS curve will cause it to shift and a change in any of the factors underlying the LM curve will cause it to shift. Figure 2-5 shows what the consequences of such shifts will be. Panel (a) deals with the consequences of shifts of the IS curve, and, as will be seen readily enough, should the curve shift upward and to the right from $I_0 S_0$ to $I_1 S_1$ the equilibrium level of income and the equilibrium level of the rate of interest will both increase. Should the curve shift to the left from $I_0 S_0$ to $I_2 S_2$ the effect is precisely opposite. If the LM curve shifts to the right from $L_0 M_0$ to $L_1 M_1$ then the level of income rises while the rate of interest falls, as may be seen by inspecting Fig. 2-5(b). A shift to the left of this curve from $L_0 M_0$ to $L_2 M_2$ has precisely the opposite effect.

If these are the effects of shifts in the IS and LM curves, what are the causes? Let us consider the IS curve first; a glance back at Fig. 2-2 will be helpful at this stage, since it is there that the derivation of this curve is shown. It will be recalled that the relationship in question between the rate of interest and the level of income is generated because investment is a component of aggregate expenditure, and because it increases as the rate of interest falls. Every point on the IS curve involves a given rate of interest generating a certain level of aggregate expenditure. If the IS curve is to shift, it means that this relationship between the level of aggregate expenditure and the rate of interest must shift. Three factors can be the cause. If the relationship between the rate of interest and the level of investment shifts to the right, it implies a higher level of aggregate expenditure at any level

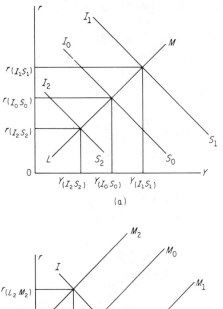

(a)

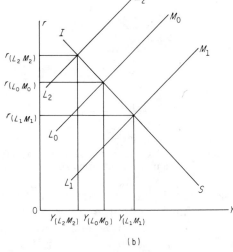

(b)

Fig. 2-5. The effect on the equilibrium
level of income and the rate of interest
of shifting the *IS* curve and the *LM*
curve.

of the rate of interest, so that the *IS* curve shifts to the right as is
shown in Fig. 2-6. A similar argument obviously follows in reverse.
If the level of government expenditure increases, then again the level
of aggregate expenditure increases for any given level of the rate of
interest so that the *IS* curve shifts to the right again. A cut in government expenditure has an opposite effect as should again be obvious.
Figure 2-7 shows this.

    The effect of a shift in the relationship between consumption and

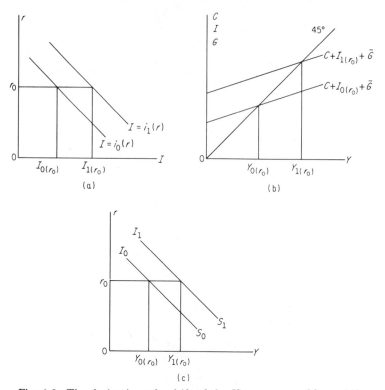

Fig. 2-6. The derivation of a shift of the IS curve caused by a shift
of the investment function.

income needs looking at with a little care, since it is by way of shifting the consumption function that taxes have their effect on the
economy. Recall that consumption depends upon disposable income,
and consider Fig. 2-8(a), in which taxes are initially assumed to be
zero so that the consumption function is first given by $C = c(Y)$. If a
tax of a fixed amount T is now levied, the level of income Y_0 will
correspond to disposable income of $(Y_0 - T)$ and consumption will
now be equal to $c(Y_0 - T)$. A similar argument will hold for any
level of income. In the presence of a tax, the consumption function
must be shifted to the right to $C = c(Y - T)$ by the amount of the tax
in order that it will still enable us to determine the level of consumption given the level of before-tax income. This is equivalent to shifting the consumption function downward by an amount equal to the
marginal propensity to consume times the amount of the tax, as
should be clear from inspection of Fig. 2-8.

In general, an increase in taxes shifts the consumption function
downward and a cut in taxes shifts it up—shifting the aggregate ex-

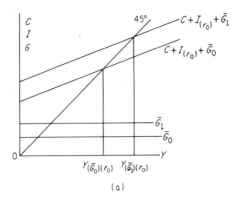

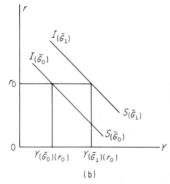

Fig. 2-7. The derivation of a shift of the IS curve caused by a change in the level of government expenditure. $(G_1 > G_0)$.

penditure curve in the same direction and by the same amount. Thus an increase in taxes shifts the IS curve to the left, while a cut in taxes shifts it to the right. Although we have here discussed cuts in the *amount* of taxes, the same conclusions follow as far as alteration in tax *rates* are concerned. A change in a tax rate may always be converted into a change in the amount of taxes paid by multiplying the change in the rate by the level of income. The only change here is that the shift in the consumption function is no longer a parallel one. This is shown in Fig. 2-8(b).

Anything that can shift the aggregate expenditure curve upward shifts the IS curve to the right, with consequences for the level of income and the rate of interest that are shown in Fig. 2-5(a). Let us now see what can cause shifts in the LM curve. As the reader might guess, since the LM curve is derived from a given demand-for-money function with a given supply of money and a given price level, a

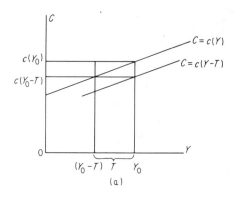

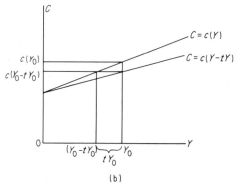

Fig. 2-8. The effect on the consumption function of introducing (a) a fixed level of taxation T and (b) proportional taxation at the rate t. Note that a change in taxes is equal to an opposite change in disposable income so that its effect on consumption at a given level of national income is to change it by the marginal propensity to consume times the change in taxes.

change in any of these factors can cause it to shift. Consider changes in the supply of money first of all. Figure 2-9(a) is similar to Fig. 2-3(b), and it should readily be seen that a change in the money supply from M_{s_0} to M_{s_1} will involve equilibria in the money market that require a lower interest rate for any given level of income. This is reflected in Fig. 2-9(b) in a shift of the LM curve from $L_0 M_0$ to $L_1 M_1$. By exactly similar reasoning, it can be shown that a cut in the money supply will shift the LM curve to the left.

Consider the next movements in the price level. It should be clear that, given the money supply, a fall in the price level will shift the LM curve to the right because this has the same effect on the

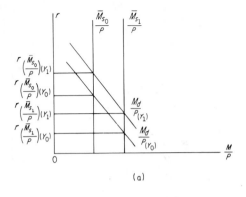

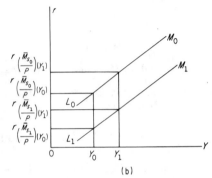

Fig. 2-9. The derivation of a shift of
the LM curve caused by an increase
in the money supply.

stock of money measured in real terms as does increasing the nominal
supply of money at a given price level. It should be equally clear that
the mechanism will work exactly in reverse in the case of an increase
in the price level. This factor becomes important when we deal with
the model in a full-employment context.

Consider finally shifts in the money demand functions. Such
changes are, of course, outside the control of the monetary authorities and therefore cannot be made an instrument of policy. But, as
we shall see later, the stability of this demand function is called into
question and an absence of stability could be an important contribu-
tor to the uncertainty underlying interest rate risk.[8] The money demand schedules in Fig. 2-10(a), differ in important respects from the
apparently similar ones depicted in Fig. 2-3(b). The latter schedules
are drawn for different levels of income, whereas, for the former, the

---

[8] The instability involved in the Keynesian speculative demand for money is
discussed below. See Chapter 6, pages 136 and following.

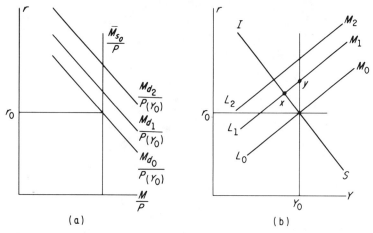

Fig. 2-10. The impact of shifts in the demand for money on the equilibrium levels of the interest rate and income. The intersection of the IS and $L_0 M_0$ curves determines the initial equilibrium level of the interest rate r_0, and income, Y_0. $\bar{M}_{s_0}$ is the nominal money stock and $M_{d_0}/P_{(Y_0)}$ is the initial money demand schedule.

level of income is the same for each. What, then, do such shifts imply for interest rates?

Given the supply of money, M_{s_0}, shifts in the demand for money schedules will require different levels of the interest rate for each level of income to insure that the same level of real balances is held. Were the interest rate not permitted to reach the level which maintains constant desired real balances—the determination of the interest rate depends on factors other than the demand for money as we have just seen—different levels of real balances would be desired which, given the nominal money stock, would lead to changes in the price level. Thus, as the demand for money shifts upward from $M_{d_0}/P_{(Y_0)}$ to $M_{d_1}/P_{(Y_0)}$ and to $M_{d_2}/P_{(Y_0)}$, as in panel (a) of Fig. 2-10, rather than producing a single LM curve showing alternative equilibrium interest rates and income levels, as in Fig. 2-3(c), alternative LM curves are generated, as in Fig. 2-10(b), higher curves corresponding to higher levels of the money demand schedule. When combined with a given IS curve, the particular equilibrium interest rates will be higher than initially, but not enough higher to keep the price level from falling. This will also cause the levels of income to be lower. To illustrate, the equilibrium level of the interest rate and income would be given by the intersection of $L_1 M_1$, and the IS curve at x rather than the intersection of $L_1 M_1$, and the vertical line over Y_0 at y.[9]

[9] An increase in the money supply sufficient to lower the interest rate to level given by x in Panel (b) would keep the price level from falling.

It is worth repeating that we are less interested in the particular shape of the *IS* and *LM* curves than in the relative instability of the various functions which underlie these curves. Thus we shall have occasion to pursue the questions surrounding the stability of the demand for money relative to that of the aggregate function. For the moment, we shall assume that the *IS* curve is negatively sloped and the *LM* curve is positively sloped so that we may consider the impact monetary and fiscal policy have on the interest rate. It will be convenient to consider this impact in two steps; first, what happens when the economy is at less than full employment and second, what happens when the economy is fully employed.

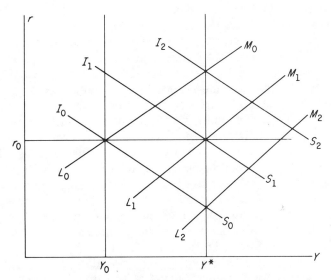

Fig. 2-11. The effect of alternative mixes of fiscal and monetary policy on the equilibrium level of the interest rate. I_0S_0 and L_0M_0 represent fiscal and monetary policy if no action is taken to move from less than full employment income Y_0 to full employment Y^*. The other *IS* and *LM* curves represent different combinations of fiscal and monetary policy actions.

In Fig. 2-11 the level of income Y_0, consistent with the underlying real variables—the consumption and investment functions—and the money demand function is less than full employment income Y^*, the price level being given. To achieve full employment it is necessary to find a way to move the economy from Y_0 to Y^* in the coming period. This can be achieved by some combination of government ex-

penditure and taxation policies that would shift the IS curve rightward and monetary policy that would shift the LM curve rightward.[10]

If the entire burden falls to fiscal policy, Y^* would be achieved
by shifting to the intersection of $I_2 S_2$ and $L_0 M_0$ which would raise
the interest rate above r_0. If the entire burden fell to monetary
policy, the money stock would be increased to shift the LM curve to
the intersection of $L_2 M_2$ and $I_0 S_0$ which would lower the interest
rate below r_0. If both fiscal and monetary policy were used, both
the IS and LM would shift to, say, the intersection of $I_1 S_1$, and
$L_1 M_1$. Whether the new rate would be higher or lower than it would
have been in the absence of policy action at the intersection of $I_0 S_0$
and $L_0 M_0$ depends on a detailed knowledge of all the functions involved. Consequently, no general statement about interest rates and
combined policy actions can be made.

As was noted earlier, the interest rate in the income expenditure
is a short-term, or better, one-period rate. What the impact of policy
actions would be on future short-run equilibrium rates remains a
question to be answered below. Recalling that, under conditions of
certainty—and this income-expenditure model resembles rather
closely the classical model in its treatment of uncertainty[11]—long-term
rates are the geometric means of the intervening, successive one-
period rates, the answer to this question depends on the impact of
current policy actions on one-period rates in future periods. Because
the present model is focused on short-run problems it does not lend
itself readily to the explicit treatment of future consumption, investment and money demand functions, though there is no reason why
we cannot use the classical model as a guide and ask what impact
current policy action could have on these functions in future periods
and hence upon one-period rates in the future.

To illustrate, pure fiscal policy, by depending heavily on government expenditure, will induce a level of private investment expenditure different from that induced by pure monetary policy, the differences depending on how firms react to increases in demand for

---

[10] When government expenditures exceed taxes, deficit financing is required.
The sales of bonds to finance the deficit has different implications from printing
money (the sale of bonds to the central bank rather than the public). We abstract here from these monetary aspects of fiscal policy.

[11] By making the IS and LM curve well defined functions producing a single
valued equilibrium interest rate and income, we are continuing to assume that
the future is known with certainty, even though the money demand function can
be rationalized fully only by assuming that the future is in some way uncertain.
In some analysis, exogenous shifts in the investment function shift the IS curve
to move the system away from full employment and such shifts are not consistent with perfect certainty. Bringing in uncertainty through the back door begs
important questions, as we shall see.

output as compared to a decrease in the interest rate. Without attempting to elaborate here, whatever mix of policy action taken, the consequences will be complex and depend, among other things, on what firms and households expect them to be. Clearly, we are on dangerous ground if we ignore these implications of expectations, but to include them here requires an explicit recognition of uncertainty.

So long as we restrict the analysis to unemployment situations it is reasonable enough to suppose that increases in the demand for goods will result in increases in output rather than price changes, and it is also useful to assume that, over the short-time periods for which this model is relevant, the existence of unemployed resources does not cause their prices, and hence the prices of the goods into whose production they enter, to fall. However, the assumption of a given price level is not so sensible at full employment, for here, were the effective demand for goods and services to be in excess of what can be produced in the short run, it seems reasonable to suppose that the result would be a bidding up of prices for those goods. Once we begin to expand the model's field of application to full employment situations, the assumption of a given price level must be modified to one of a price level that does not fall, but will rise in the presence of an excess demand for goods and services at full employment. Indeed it is precisely the effect on the money market of such a rising price level that rids the economy of excess demand and brings it to equilibrium.

In terms of the analytic framework in which we are working, such a situation of excess demand arises when the LM and IS curves intersect at a level of income that is higher than the maximum that can be produced in the short run. This latter level of income is given as Y^* in Fig. 2-12. In a situation of excess demand the price level is bid up from its initial value of P_0, and as this happens the supply of money measured in real terms falls and the LM curve begins to shift to the left. So long as excess demand persists, this process continues. It ceases when the price level has risen sufficiently to make the quantity of money measured in real terms compatible with the demand for it at Y^* and at the level of the interest rate which conditions in real-goods market require for equilibrium at Y^*. This occurs when the LM curve has shifted far enough to intersect the IS curve at Y^*. At this point the model is back in equilibrium with a price level of P_1 as is shown in Fig. 2-12.

This extension of the model to full-employment situations enables us to say a little more than previously about the effects of various changes on the economy. Everything said earlier holds true so

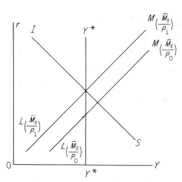

Fig. 2-12. The effect on the
LM curve of a price rise
brought about by an initial
situation of excess demand.
Y^* is the highest level of income that can be attained
$(P_1 > P_0)$.

long as we deal with unemployment situations. However, if we start
out from a situation of full-employment equilibrium it is clear that
the policy actions involve increases in the level of income that cannot
be brought about. In Fig. 2-13(a) the shift of the *IS* curve so that it
intersects the *LM* curve at the right of Y^* sets in motion a price rise
from P_0 that causes the *LM* curve to shift to the left. The consequence of the shift is ultimately a higher price level P_1 and a higher
rate of interest rather than a higher level of income and a higher rate
of interest as in the unemployment case. Similarly, the shift to the
right of the *LM* curve displayed in Fig. 2-13(b), caused by an increase
in the money supply from M_{s_0} to M_{s_1}, creates an excess demand for
goods that results in the price level rising from P_0 until at P_1 the
money supply measured in real terms is again compatible with
equilibrium—that is, takes the same value as it did initially. In this
case the price level must move in proportion to the money supply
while the rate of interest remains unchanged.

In Fig. 2-13(a) the initial tendency for an increase in expenditure, either public or private, is restrained by an increase in the interest rate.[12] If the expansion came from an increase in government expenditures, private investment expenditures must decline to free
resources for the government. If the initial impulse was due to a
rightward shift in the aggregate investment function, the higher interest rate serves to keep actual expenditures unchanged by increasing
opportunity costs to firms. In either case, the one-period rate as well

[12] The impact of taxes is ignored here for simplicity.

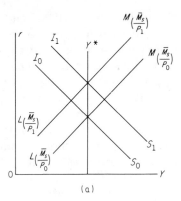

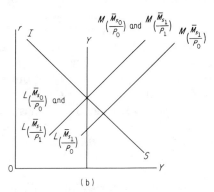

Fig. 2-13. The effect of excess demand brought about by (a) a shift of the IS curve and (b) a shift of the LM curve

$$\left(M_{s_1} > M_{s_0}, P_1 > P_0, \frac{M_{s_1}}{P_1} = \frac{M_{s_0}}{P_0}\right).$$

as the price level has risen. We may now ask what the impact of these shifts will be on subsequent one-period rates and hence on longer-term rates.

Long-term rates will rise, of course, because the current one-period rate is an element in them. But what of future one-period rates? Recalling the classical model in which a series of successive supply and demand schedules for loanable funds can be treated explicitly, the answer can be seen to depend on the shifts induced in these schedules by the shifts in the current IS curve. If the intersection of these schedules in future periods shift upward, long-term rates will rise even further. However, how these intersections will move is an empirical matter, involving not only the behavior of the real variable involved but also the way in which firms and households form their expectations. We shall return to these matters later. With regard to the change in the price level, if it was a once for all shift, it cannot make nominal and real interest rates diverge.

Turning to panel (b), we can see that a purely monetary phenomenon cannot permanently affect the real rate of interest, including current and future one-period rates, when the nominal money is increased by a fixed amount in a single step. The initial lowering of the interest rate caused by the increase in the nominal money stock is reversed as the short-run equilibrium is reached. The absence of a purely monetary impact accords with the conclusions for the classical model. However, once we move to a situation of continuous increases in the nominal money stock which produce a continuing inflation, the impact on successive one-period rates becomes a matter for inquiry. If it is generally understood that a policy of continuous inflation has been adopted, financial contracts written in nominal terms will reflect the declining purchasing power of money. As before, the real rate will not be affected by a purely monetary phenomenon. As a consequence, long-term nominal rates will exceed future real one-period rates. It should be emphasized that this divergence of nominal and real rates occurs when inflation is anticipated. However, it is difficult to discuss fully the problem arising under unanticipated inflation without explicitly introducing uncertainty. We will return to this problem later.

The major objective of the foregoing analysis was to provide a means to link theories of the term structure that will be reviewed below to an eclectic, but widely accepted, theory of interest rate determination. By identifying the principal variables that influence the level of "the interest rate" it will be possible to give a more satisfactory focus to the problems of portfolio management, including especially the variables portfolio managers must forecast, and thereby gaining a clearer understanding of the processes by which the term structure of interest rates is determined. This understanding is necessary to achieve a useful perspective on the implications of recent work in this area for the conduct of stabilization policy. It should be noted that the principal area of policy of concern here, the maturity composition of U.S. Government debt, cannot be treated in the rather simple macroeconomic model set forth here. The necessary complications will be introduced later.

It may be useful at this point to list these key variables, noting that accurate forecasts of the course of interest rates requires that portfolio managers know a great deal more about them than is contained in the analysis of their relationship presented above. It is perhaps important to emphasize that it is not necessary to show here how interest rate forecasting might be done: rather it is sufficient for our purposes to spell out in a fairly rigorous way what is involved in linking the conventional variables of interest theory to theories of how interest rate structures are determined.

Factors Influencing the Level of the Interest Rate

1. Variables usually taken as given in comparative static analysis but which are subject to change.[13]
   a. population
   b. demographic characteristic of population, including the stock of human capital
   c. technology
2. Variables traditionally considered important
   a. productivity—investment opportunities open to firms
   b. thrift—preferences of households for future over present consumption
3. Policy variables
   a. nominal money stock
   b. government expenditures
   c. taxes

Having come this far, it is necessary to confront directly the problems posed by explicitly relaxing the assumption of perfect certainty. Clearly, none of the variables in the above list can be known with certainty and estimates of them can come to influence interest rates only through the mediation of portfolio managers who transact business in the market on the basis of imperfect forecasts of them. In the next chapter we attempt to take uncertainty into account directly.

[13] A word on the terminology used so far may help to clarify what is meant by the possibility of change in these underlying variables. Both long-run and short-run equilibria in the classical world, and the short-run equilibria in the income-expenditure world take these variables as given. The distinction between long and short-run turned on whether or not the capital stock changed, but not on whether these other variables changed. Looking ahead, a more useful distinction will be between long and short-term time horizons during which changes in the underlying variables may occur. While it would be cumbersome to work out fully the implications of such changes for both short- and long-run static equilibria, it should be clear that changes of this kind will produce shifts in equilibrium one-period interest rates. Certain general features of such changes which relate time horizons to the term structure will be developed below. It will be seen there that chronological time rather than the analytical time of comparative static analysis plays the primary role.

chapter 3

Taking Uncertainty into Account

The income-expenditure model presented in the preceding chapter did not provide a systematic treatment of uncertainty. As was noted, in a number of ways it did not differ from the classical model with its explicit assumption of perfect certainty. Yet the possibility of disequilibria is inconsistent with this assumption. In this chapter we relax this assumption. We shall be concerned mainly with two implications of this relaxation. First, we shall explore its impact on the interpretations to be given observed yields to maturity since these arise under conditions of uncertainty. And, second, given that we have gained an understanding of the way the private financial sector responds to uncertainty, we shall explore what this understanding means for the conduct of stabilization policy.

A. MODELS OF PORTFOLIO MANAGEMENT

1. The Certainty Case

In the stationary-state equilibrium there is no portfolio management problem, nor is there a need for financial intermediaries. All securities are perpetuities and all that is required is a means for retiring households to exchange their holdings for the cash provided by the savings of younger households out of their current income. The yield curve will be flat since the interest rate remains constant.[1] A simple brokerage arrangement could facilitate the necessary exchange and we will ignore its cost here. However, once we make allowance for short-run disequilibria we find the need to introduce financial

---

[1] Though, as was shown in Chapter 1, prior to the stationary stable equilibrium the yield curve could slope upward or downward. If there is only one kind of perpetuity—one with periodic payments—only one market yield could be observed.

intermediaries and to recognize that institutional portfolios and their management must be explicitly taken into account. Monetary policy works through a fractional reserve commercial banking system and banks hold portfolios which include risky as well as default-free assets. The relationship between the risk of default and interest rate risk remains quite unclear in the literature on the term structure and on stabilization policy. In this chapter I set out a model which links them explicitly through the medium of portfolio management.

It will be helpful in moving toward a systematic treatment of the impact of uncertainty to begin with a model of institutional port-folio management under certainty. While, as we have just seen, such a model is something of a contradiction in terms, it will nevertheless serve to highlight the crucial aspects of the uncertainty case. Consider, then, that all households hold claims on financial intermediaries which in turn hold the perpetuities issued by the corporate sector. What would the problem of portfolio management be like for such intermediaries?

Consider first the characteristics of intermediary liabilities and the management problem they would impose. Suppose households save by purchasing intermediary deposits of fixed maturities according to a schedule of their retirement needs. At any point in time the intermediary will have a maturity distribution of liabilities. But, as we have seen, in the stationary state this distribution will remain stable over time since, from a stable population, outflows of cash will be exactly matched by inflows. Consequently, liabilities pose no management problems. In particular, the asset portfolio can be entirely composed of perpetuities since the only cash drain on the assets will be met by periodic interest payments which are used to meet interest due on liabilities.

Asset management poses no problem. All perpetuities are riskless. Portfolio selection involves acquiring perpetuities once and for all. Not only do individual securities have indefinite lives but the asset portfolio itself has an indefinite life. This is a point of fundamental significance. Individual households have finite lives and correspondingly will have needs for cash at fixed dates. But this is not true of financial intermediaries. Intermediaries must be regarded as perpetual funds engaged in a continuing process of portfolio management. Under conditions of certainty, once equilibrium is reached, the process entails no effort or cost. However, once uncertainty is introduced, information about the future becomes costly, forecasting becomes necessary and continuing efforts to deal with the effects of unforeseen changes, including the development of strategies for coping with changes, becomes the central feature of portfolio management. As I shall try to show later, most writers concerned with the term structure have taken the household with its finite life and specific needs as the model of institutional portfolio management. This household analogy has had unfortunate consequences.

2. The Uncertainty Case

A rigorous specification of risk and uncertainty and how they differ will be presented shortly. For the present let us consider the implications of the circumstance that disturbances to the steady-state equilibrium are possible. The possibility of such disturbances means that the future cannot be known once and for all with perfect certainty. Consequently, effort must be expended to forecast the future as a means of coping with disequilibria as they arise. The collection and processing of information for this purpose is costly. Forecasting is an imperfect art. Because forecasts can go wrong and because information will become available with the passage of time, portfolio management becomes a continuous process involving collection of information, preparation of forecasts, and review of past decisions and adjustments in the light of the evaluation of performance. Moreover, in contrast to the once and for all selection decision under certainty, the recognition of the continuous character of portfolio management under uncertainty opens up the possibility of strategic behavior.

Strategic behavior arises when information is costly—which is to say when the future is uncertain—because some market participants may be more efficient than others in acquiring new information and in using such information once acquired. Perhaps the most common characterization of differences in portfolio strategies arising because of such differentials in information processing capacity is the hedger-speculator dichotomy. According to this view, market participants either seek to avoid the consequences of disturbances because they cannot anticipate them—that is, hedge—or seek to gain from these consequences by anticipating them—that is, speculate. This dichotomy is usually taken, rather casually, as an accurate or at least satisfactory account of the objectives of portfolio managers. However, it has very serious limitations and has held back proper understanding of private sector portfolio management.

One way to see the limitations involved in the conventional notion of a hedging strategy is to consider the impact of uncertainty on the management of liabilities both for a household and for a financial intermediary. Let us continue to assume that a household's assets will be the liabilities of financial intermediaries the assets of which are perpetuities issued by the corporate sector. As the household retires it will sell its assets to meet living expenses: that is, it will have "need" for cash at fixed dates. This finite horizon stems from its finite life—once its working life is over, income flows cease. If the household has arranged to hold assets which mature at the exact time and in the proper amount, unanticipated changes in the interest rate will not affect its pattern of consumption in retirement.

To see what might have happened in the absence of hedging, assume that the household had held perpetuities directly rather than the dated liabilities of an intermediary. Suppose, further, that the level of interest rates had risen and that this rise was not generally anticipated. As will be developed more fully later, this change in the level of rates would produce windfall price declines in perpetuities.[2] As the household came to sell perpetuities to meet its consumption needs it would find that cash proceeds from the sale of a given proportion of its asset holdings were less than anticipated. Further, because it cannot borrow against future income, there being none, it will find that it must reduce its level of consumption. This adjustment can be avoided by holding assets which mature on the dates cash is needed: that is, by hedging. Unanticipated changes in the interest rate cannot alter nominal face values.

The financial intermediary has no similar reason to avoid the consequences of interest rate changes. Under conditions of certainty, cash inflows and outflows arising from its liabilities exactly balance so that no management problem exists. Under uncertainty, inflows may be greater or less than outflows, which possible imbalance imposes the need to coordinate asset management with liability management. Because it can meet drains when outflows exceed inflows by reducing its asset holdings and, conversely, accumulate assets when inflows exceed outflows, the intermediary has no fixed or irreducible needs, such as befalls the retired household when its labor income ceases, to protect by hedging.

The intermediary is thus in a position to adopt a strategy to cope with disturbances in ways that could lead to profits. It can decide how much of the risk associated with shifts in the level of interest rates it is willing to bear. As part of bearing this risk it must develop a means of collecting information on the variables that affect the level of the interest rate so that it is in a position to forecast changes in the interest rate. If it can successfully forecast, the intermediary can capture speculative profits; if it cannot, it will forgo these and suffer the consequences of adverse changes in rates. Only by engag-

---

[2] For example consider a perpetuity yielding $50 per annum. If the market yield is 5 percent, its price will be $1,000. If the market yield rises to 6 percent—that is, if all successive one-period rates rise to 6 percent—the price will fall to $833. This is a matter of arithmetic if we are correct in assuming that all successive one-period rates increase one percentage point. We shall see later that what happens when rates change is an empirical not a logical matter.

ing in a forecasting effort can the intermediary make judgments
about the rewards for bearing risk and establish the trade-offs between risk and return.

It will be helpful before turning to a closer examination of the
strategic considerations involved in making these judgments, to de-
lineate more precisely what is involved in the idea of uncertainty and
how this bears on interest rate risk.

B. RISK, UNCERTAINTY, AND FORECASTING

So far we have seen that portfolio management under conditions
other than certainty can become quite complex. To keep this complexity from turning to confusion, some carefully specified conceptual models of portfolio management under different kinds of departure from certainty are needed. These models will prove useful for
the critical review of the term structure literature which follows in
later chapters.

A recent treatment of risk and uncertainty by Cohen and Cyert
provides a number of distinctions which are useful in making clear
the shortcomings of the hedger-speculator dichotomy as it is commonly applied to models of institutional portfolio management.[3]
They distinguish four principal states of knowledge about the future:
certainty, objective risk, subjective risk, and uncertainty. The chief
distinction between these states turns on the characteristics of the
information available to the decision makers. Under certainty the
probability attached to estimates of future events is 1.0; that is, the
estimates are certain. Under objective risk, the probabilities are less
than 1.0 but are known to all market participants. Under subjective
risk, the probabilities are themselves estimates and consequently
differ among decisionmakers. Under uncertainty, there are gaps in
these subjective estimates; that is, the participants know their
estimates do not cover the entire field.

The notion of objectively known probabilities is a problematical
one. An example of such might be the probabilities used by actuaries to construct mortality tables for computing life insurance
premiums. Rather than arguing the point at length, let me assert that
portfolio managers cannot rely on past experience to derive probabilities in the same way actuaries can.[4] For our purposes it will be more

---

[3] See [11, pp. 307–309].

[4] The position taken here is Bayesian; namely, that decision makers have
some a priori notion of probabilities from which to begin. As information arises
in the process of making decisions the initial probability distribution will usually
be altered. There is no independent, objective way to determine the "true"
probabilities. See [57] for a full discussion.

helpful to consider all probabilities as subjective estimates based on whatever past experience and present information is available. We may then define a state of objective risk as one in which these subjective estimates are uniform among market participants. Under subjective risk these estimates diverge. And finally, under uncertainty, these estimates not only diverge but have major gaps because of the novelty inherent in the future. Novelty means that even though expenditures on forecasting can reduce ignorance about the future, perfect certainty is not attainable.

It is useful to distinguish, as Cohen and Cyert do, between the situation in which the portfolio manager (or decision maker in their terms) has probability estimates for all opportunities and those in which gaps in these estimates exist.[5] Indeed, once we recognize that the collection and processing of information is costly, some notion corresponding to this incompleteness is essential. However, it is misleading to make uncertainty refer in this way to a particular state of information on opportunities at a point in time. In what follows, risk, objective and subjective, with or without gaps, will denote a characteristic of the state of the available information at a point in time. Uncertainty will refer to the circumstance that the passage of time can bring with it changes in the information; that is, some new opportunities or variations in old ones not previously taken into account. Thus, interest rate risk exists at a point in time because the projected course of interest rates can change in unexpected ways; that is, the course of rates is uncertain.

Given these ways in which to characterize the information available to portfolio managers, we can use them to develop a model of portfolio management under uncertainty. We begin with a simple one-asset model of default risk and then proceed to the two-asset case to show how portfolio diversification can be taken into account. The many-asset case is then presented as a model of market equilibrium under conditions of objective risk. Because it limits portfolio management to diversification at a point in time, this equilibrium model makes it quite clear that two factors are essential to understanding interest rate risk: the passage of time and the possibility of

[5] One way to treat gaps in a classificatory scheme of this kind is to say the probability estimates are unknown. The notion of probability estimates is expanded below to the notion of probability distributions for investment outcomes. Gaps in this context would mean that, because of the lack of information, probability densities are uniform. Thus, at any point in time, gaps create no special problem because formally all opportunities have some probability distribution associated with them. What is crucial here is to recognize that the passage of time will necessarily bring new information when there are gaps, but need not if there were no gaps. Thus, the existence of gaps means the system is dynamically unstable or, alternatively, is nonstationary.

unforeseen events it gives rise to. The chapter closes with a consideration of the implications of the passage of time for portfolio management.

1. Risk and the Individual Portfolio

Consider a perpetuity (say, a share of common stock) issued by Firm A selling at time 0 at V_{a_0}. Its price at time 1, the end of an arbitrarily selected period of time, may be described by the parameters of a probability distribution V_{a_1} and $\sigma_{V_{a_1}}$, the mean and standard deviation respectively.   Assume also that the portfolio manager in question has acquired the information on these parameters at no cost.   Define possible rates of return on the perpetuity as follows:

$$(3\text{-}1) \qquad\qquad r_a = \log\left(\frac{V_{a_1}}{V_{a_0}}\right)$$

the expected rate of return or yield, $\hat{r}_{a_1}$, is the expected value of the distribution of the r_{a_1}, given that the distribution of the V_{a_1} is lognormal.   It will be convenient to assume lognormality because the distribution of the logarithm of the ratio of lognormally distributed variables is normal.[6]   Normal distributions can be completely described by their means and standard deviations; in this instance, by $\hat{r}_{a_1}$ and $\sigma_{r_{a_1}}$.   By keeping to these statistical ideas we can keep our discussion simple and make use of two-dimensional diagrams.   This should cause no harm as long as we keep in mind that our purpose in doing so is a heuristic one.

To help do this, let us take note that this definition of risk is a convention, albeit a widely adopted one. It can be easily adapted to represent certainty—the standard deviation of possible returns to a default-free perpetuity being zero. As we shall see, this property is not necessarily a virtue. The larger is the σ_{r_a}, the greater the risk. A portfolio containing only shares in Firm A would possess expected yield and risk characteristics, $\hat{r}_a$, σ_{r_a}. Let us now consider the possi-

---

[6] If Eq. 3-1 is expressed in natural logarithms and properly scaled it can provide an approximation to continuous annual rate of change of price. The expected value would then simply be an interest rate in per annum dimensions. When analyzing price data it is helpful to have the data expressed in commonly used dimensions as will be evident below.   Further, growth is a multiplicative process, not an additive one. If it were a stable process subject to the central limit thereon, it would be normal in the logarithms, since logarithm convert multiplication to addition.   In fact, time series data do not appear to be normally distributed.   The implications of this nonnormality is discussed in Chapter 4.

bilities for reducing the risk on a portfolio by diversification. First, assume an additional perpetuity, issued by Firm B, having yield and risk characteristics $\hat{r}_b$ and σ_{r_b}. These two investment opportunities are represented by points a and b in Fig. 3-1. We may ask what possible combinations of yield and risk are available on portfolios containing various proportions of the two financial assets.

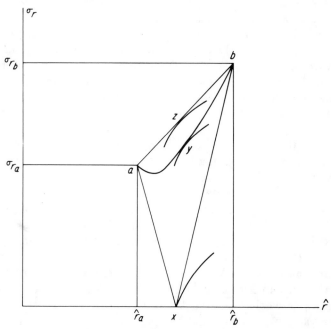

Fig. 3-1. Portfolio opportunities for the two asset case for alternative degrees of correlation between the distributions of returns to the two assets. $\hat{r}$ is expected yield, σ_r is risk, points a and b represent the expected yield and risk characteristics of asset A and B respectively.

To answer this, consider a portfolio composed of α of asset A and $(1 - \alpha)$ of asset B, $0 \leqslant \alpha \leqslant 1$. The expected yield on the combination of assets will be

$$(3\text{-}2) \qquad\qquad \hat{r}_c = \alpha \hat{r}_a + (1 - \alpha) \hat{r}_b$$

The risk on the combination will be

$$(3\text{-}3) \qquad \sigma_{r_c} = \sqrt{\alpha^2 \, \sigma_{r_a}^2 + (1 - \alpha)^2 \, \sigma_{r_b}^2 + 2\rho_{ab} \, \alpha \, (1 - \alpha) \, \sigma_{r_a} \sigma_{r_b}}$$

Risk on the portfolio includes the correlation coefficient ρ_{ab} reflecting the degree interdependence of the prospects of the two firms. Since ρ_{ab} can in principle range from -1 to 1, the risk on the combination can be less than the risk on a portfolio containing either all asset A or asset B.

Consider the situation when $\rho_{ab} = 1$. For example, suppose that both assets are identical claims on the same firm. Not very realistic, to be sure, since the prospects of very few if any enterprises are likely to be perfectly correlated. In this instance ρ_{ab} becomes unity so that σ_{r_c} becomes $\alpha\sigma_{r_a} + (1 - \alpha)\sigma_{r_b}$;[7] that is, the risk on the combination is simply the weighted average of the risk on the two assets taken separately. This relationship is depicted by the straight line azb.

Should ρ_{ab} be exactly minus unity some α could be found such that risk on one asset just offsets the risk on the other which in Eq. (3-3) would mean that, because $\rho_{ab} < 0$, the last term on the right-hand side canceled the other two terms. Again, hardly a realistic situation. This situation is depicted by line segments ax and xb. The more likely case is that in which $-1 < \rho_{ab} < 1$ and, most likely, $0 < \rho_{ab} < 1$; that is, there is some tendency for prospects for individual assets to move together during major market swings.[8] This situation is depicted by curve ayb.[9]

Once there are a number of alternatives or, put differently, once the opportunity set contains more than one option—the positively sloped portions of the three opportunity sets depicted in Fig. 3-1— some mechanism leading to a choice among the options becomes necessary. The mechanism used here, and which will be amplified more fully later, is the Von Neumann-Morgenstern utility function presented below in Fig. 3-2.[10] The vertical axis measures utility, the horizontal axis wealth. Curve 1 represents the relationship between the utility and wealth of a market participant averse to risk. Thus, utility rises less rapidly than wealth and conversely declines more rapidly.

---

[7] If ρ_{ab} is unity, the right-hand term on the right side of Eq. 3-3 becomes simply the cross product from squaring the sum $\alpha\sigma_{r_a} + (1 - \alpha)\sigma_{r_b}$; namely, 2α $(1 - \alpha)\sigma_{r_a}\sigma_{r_b}$. All points lying on a straight line in this kind of risk-return diagram must represent perfectly correlated portfolios.

[8] Sharpe [59, pp. 439–440] interprets the tendency as arising from the forces producing cyclical movements in economic activity. Business cycles appear as cycles after the fact; this should not be permitted to obscure their disequilibrium character. They cannot be predicted by any simple extrapolation from past cycles which take them as generated by a stationary process. This interpretation combined with a static equilibrium model of security markets tends to mask the nonstationary character of interest rate risk as we shall see.

[9] When the correlation coefficient is less than unity but greater than minus unity, the cross product described in footnote 7 does not behave in linear fashion.

[10] A helpful discussion of utility functions can be found in Baumol [3, pp. 536–552].

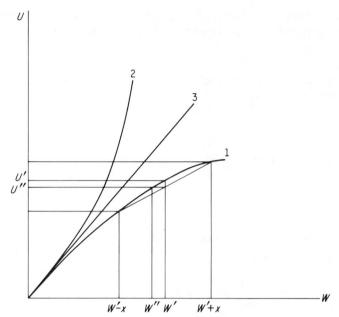

Fig. 3-2. Three possible utility functions showing the relationship between wealth, W and utility, U. Risk aversion is depicted by curve 1, risk preference by curve 2, and indifference to risk by curve 3.

To see what this means consider a portfolio manager responsible for a portfolio worth W' who has an option of paying X for a .5 of winning $2X$ and .5 chance of losing the purchase price. The expected wealth of this option is exactly W'.[11] However, the expected utility, which is given by the intersection of the chord with the line perpendicular to W', U'', and is less than the utility of not buying the option which is given simply the utility function at W', U'. A risk averter will not play a fair game because it lowers his utility.[12]

By the same reasoning curve 2 represents a preference for risk and curve 3 represents an indifference to risk. We shall assume in what follows that the dominant, even the sole attitude of portfolio managers is one of aversion to risk, though the degree of aversion

---

[11] Let expected wealth be $\overline{W}'$. Then $\overline{W}' = .5\,(W' + x) + .5\,(W' - X) = W'$.

[12] He will buy insurance even though the premium exceeds its expected value. Assume the insured wealth to be $W' + X$ with a .5 chance of its being reduced to $W' - X$. This expected wealth without insurance is W' yielding utility U''. A premium that reduced his wealth to W'' would also yield utility U''. Any smaller premium than this which is greater than X will yield utility greater than U'' and still provide the insurer with a premium in excess of the expected value of policy payment which in this case would be X.

may vary among them.[13]   From utility functions like curve 1 in Fig. 3-2, indifference curves can be derived such as those depicted in Fig. 3-1. These are tangent only to positively sloped portions of the opportunity sets because risk aversion requires that increased risk be accompanied by increased yield.[14]

Before considering how the single portfolio model relates to the hedger-speculator dichotomy it will be helpful to consider the more general case of an indefinitely larger number of assets. The yield on a portfolio with a large number of assets is as before, the weighted average of the individual yields

$$(3\text{-}4) \qquad\qquad \hat{r}_c = \sum_{\alpha=1}^{N} \alpha_j \hat{r}_j$$

where N is the number of financial assets in the portfolio.

The risk is

$$(3\text{-}5) \qquad \sigma_{r_c} = \sqrt{\sum_{j=1}^{N} \alpha_j^2 \, \sigma_{r_j}^2 + 2 \sum_{j=1, j \neq k}^{N} \rho_{jk} \, \alpha_j \, \alpha_k \, \sigma_{r_j} \, \sigma_{r_k}}$$

As the number of assets N increases, the proportion of the portfolio in any one asset α_j diminishes. As a consequence, the influence of the risk on each asset $\sigma_{r_j}^2$ taken separately declines. But the impact of interrelationship of prospects between assets will not decline in this way.   The behavior of the second term on the right-hand side of Eq. 3-5 depends both on the weights α_j and on the correlation coefficients, ρ_{jk}. If the average value of the ρ_{jk} exceeds zero, and the suggestion made above that this will be so because of marketwide swings associated with movement in economic activity has been widely accepted as a rationale[15] for a residual nondiversifiable risk, portfolio risks will tend to some lower limit greater than zero. If the average

[13] It may seem somewhat peremptory to preclude the possibility of risk preference or indifference. I do not exclude these possibilities just to simplify the exposition.   Rather, casual observation seems to demonstrate overwhelmingly that in the bulk of their daily affairs men seek to reduce the impact of uncertainty. It is the daily affairs of men which concerns us here, not special situations that may arise in, say Las Vegas.

[14] The indifference curve intersecting point X in Fig. 3-1 constitutes a special case. A more likely portfolio selection when the prospects of the two assets are perfectly inverse would be to accept some risk for an increase in expected yield. Risk aversion is not the same as risk avoidance.

[15] We shall have occasion later to consider other explanations of widespread shifts in expectations. One of particular interest is that instability in expectations cause, rather than result from, shifts in economic activity. See Chapter 7, page 162.

value of ρ_{jk} is zero, individual risks, which are essentially independent of each other, will tend to cancel as the number of assets increases so that risk-free portfolios would become possible.[16] Once the numbers of available assets exceed two, the characterization of an opportunity set becomes more complicated. Figure 3-3, which follows Markowitz quite closely,[17] depicts the many-asset case. The curve *os* forms the

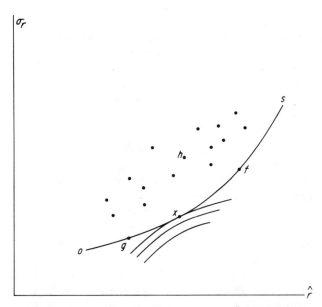

Fig. 3-3. Portfolio opportunities for the many asset case. σ_s constitutes the set of efficient portfolios for which expected yield r is a maximum for each level of risk σ_r. The portfolio at g has the same expected yield as the portfolio at h but less risk. The portfolio at f has the same risk as the portfolio at h but more expected yield.

boundary of the opportunity set and itself contains only efficient portfolios; that is, opportunities for which expected yield is maximized at each level of risk. Interior portfolios above and to the left of the boundary, such as at h, are inefficient. A portfolio manager averse to risk would always choose a portfolio on the boundary since there is only a minimum risk at each level of expected yield.

---

[16] It is not possible for the prospective returns all assets to be negatively correlated. At most there could be two classes of assets for which the correlation of returns was negative between the classes. However, as between assets in the same class, the correlation cannot be negative. Even though negative correlation of this kind is possible, there is little evidence of it.

[17] See Markowitz [41].

Deriving the efficient opportunity set in the two asset case is fairly straightforward as Eqs. 3-2 and 3-3 attest. All the alternatives lie on the efficient boundary: inefficient interior portfolios are not possible. In the many-asset case it becomes necessary to use more complex procedures to go from the characteristics of individual assets to the characteristics of efficient portfolios: many combinations of assets will be inefficient. We shall do no more here than to recognize that extensive and costly computations are required to arrive at the opportunity set depicted in Fig. 3-3.[18] We have so far ignored the problems raised by information costs, and will continue to do so for a while longer.

To assume that information on returns and the computations necessary to convert this information into an efficient opportunity set are costless is to move very cautiously indeed from conditions of perfect certainty. It will be convenient in what follows to call attention to this assumption by emphasizing its actuarial character. Thus, we will refer to the information base under this assumption as the actuarial matrix. Portfolio managers, then, have access at no cost to a matrix containing the covariance of the distributions of possible yields for all assets and a vector for the means for all distributions.[19] The actuarial matrix is converted into an efficient opportunity set at no cost. Certainty can be seen, then, simply as the special case in which all entries in the actuarial matrix are zero except those in the vector of expected yields which are identical—that is, there is only one interest rate. Stated this way, the assumption may appear somewhat stark but, in truth, this is the way information collection and processing are handled in much of the literature dealing with portfolio selection. Once the opportunity set is defined, as in Fig. 3-3, portfolio selection follows quite simply from conversion of the utility function of the portfolio manager into a family of indifference curves and finding the point of tangency as at x in Fig. 3-3.[20]

---

[18] Markowitz [41, pp. 129-144] illustrates what is involved for three assets. An extensive literature exists on the computation of efficiency. See the bibliography in Sharpe [60].

[19] The correlation coefficient measures the relationship between the covariance between two variables and their variances: thus,

$$\rho_{jk} = \text{cov}_{jk} / \sqrt{\sigma_{rj}^2 \, \sigma_{rk}^2}$$

The matrix of the kind described here will contain a row and column for every asset. The entries on the diagonal will provide the variances; the entries off the diagonal, the covariances. In addition, a vector containing the expected yields on assets is necessary. The term *actuarial matrix* describes this data base.

[20] The utility function relevant to portfolio choice for households is the household's. When the portfolio being managed is an institution's the relevant utility function is not immediately obvious. I shall argue below that institutions

This treatment of information costs effectively rules out the passage of time during which changes in information could arise. Time, as in the classical model, is in a kind of suspended steady state. Both hedging and speculative behavior entail the passage of time rather than its suspension. Consequently, we must go beyond this meager departure from certainty if we are to understand these kinds of behavior.

Moreover, no allowance can be made here for differences of opinion—an essential ingredient in speculative behavior—until more than one portfolio manager enters the market. Given two or more market participants it is not only possible for divergent views to arise but for the differences to be explicitly recognized by some of the participants and thus to make possible the ingredients for speculative strategies. These strategies and hedging (which can be considered a special kind of strategy) can best be understood in a context which includes more than one portfolio manager. To facilitate this understanding we now turn to a model of a market in financial assets.

2. Risk and Market Equilibrium

Market equilibrium under objective risk. In the preceding case current prices, the V_{j_0}, were taken as given and an opportunity set derived for a single portfolio manager based on the actuarial matrix of returns as seen by him. The question now to be answered is, given a number of portfolio managers each with his own actuarial matrix, how are current prices determined. W. Sharpe provides a very useful model for the case in which expectations are homogenous; that is, when all managers have the same actuarial matrix.[21]

What affect does the homogeneity assumption have? Consider the situation in which the current price of a particular asset V_{j_0} is arbitrarily changed. Managers now compute a new opportunity set and many, if not all, would find themselves holding inefficient portfolios. For example, our investor whose situation is depicted in Fig. 3-3 at point x would now find himself at an interior point. Managers would attempt to sell (buy) the jth asset if its price had risen (fallen) to increase expected yields and reduce risk. This would

---

have utility functions and that we may speak of the portfolio manager's preferences without distinguishing between household and institutional portfolios. It will be argued in Chapter 6 that it is entirely appropriate to use an element of the theory of household behavior—utility functions belong to consumers, not producers, in standard theory—to model institutional behavior. In particular, I will show that straightforward profit maximization cannot lead to determinate institutional decisions regarding risk bearing.

[21] See Sharpe [59].

move V_{j_0} back toward its original level and trading would continue or attempts to trade continue until the original equilibrium was restored. Thus, all managers would hold efficient portfolios. Since the actuarial matrix as well as current prices are the same for all managers, one opportunity set with identical interior points and boundary would apply to all managers. Moreover, a special relationship would hold between the yields and risk on individual assets. For any three assets, M, N and Q as shown in Fig. 3-4, such that $r_m = r_n < r_q$ and

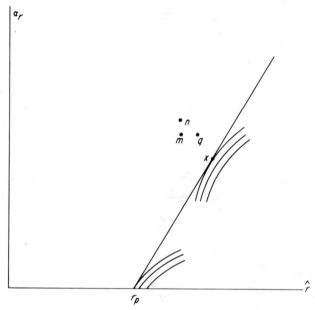

Fig. 3-4. Equilibrium in the market for financial assets under conditions of objective risk. The actuarial matrix of returns is identical for all market participants. r_p is the pure or riskless rate of interest at which borrowing and lending occur.

$\sigma_{r_q} = \sigma_{r_m} < \sigma_{r_m}$, asset N will have a lower average correlation with other assets than asset M (hence the same yield with great internal risk) and asset Q has a higher average correlation with other assets than asset M (hence a higher yield with the same internal risk).

Because it simplified the presentation of his argument Sharpe also assumed that investors can lend or borrow at the riskless rate of interest.[22] The effect of this assumption is to make the efficient op-

---

[22] For a discussion of some of the difficulties involved in depicting borrowing and lending in this kind of model when it is recognized that collateral for loans cannot be risk free see Brewer and Michaelsen [5]. As long as we keep in mind the mainly heuristic purpose of Sharpe's assumption, no harm is done by it.

portunity set linear as is shown in Fig. 3-4. To show how borrowing and lending produce this result, consider point x which corresponds to point x in Fig. 3-3, a portfolio on the curved efficient set. The intercept r_p in Fig. 3-4 represents the riskless rate of interest for which σ_{r_p} and for which all $\rho_{jp} = 0$. By holding a fraction α of riskless bonds (lending) and $1 - \alpha$ of the risky portfolio x, the expected yield becomes

$$\hat{r}_c = \alpha r_p + (1 - \alpha) \hat{r}_x$$

and the risk becomes

$$\sigma_{r_c} = \sqrt{\alpha^2 \sigma_{r_p}^2 + (1 - \alpha)^2 \sigma_{r_x}^2 + 2\rho_{xp} \alpha (1 - \alpha) \sigma_{r_x} \sigma_{r_p}}$$

which reduces to $(1 - \alpha)\sigma_{r_x}$ since both σ_{r_p} and ρ_{xp} are zero. This transforms the boundary to the ray extending from r_p to x. By similar reasoning, borrowing, using owned assets as collateral will extend the efficient set beyond point x as depicted. The efficient set is tangent to an indifference curve of every portfolio manager participating in the market and its slope reflecting the influence of risk aversion.[23]

As in the previous and simpler models just considered, the problem of portfolio management is one of initial selection. The efficient opportunity set exists in a timeless steady state having come into existence as a consequence of a prior and costless collection and processing of information leading to the same actuarial matrix for all portfolio managers. Since hedging is also a once and for all event, it might appear that the static character of the model would be useful in an analysis hedging behavior. Unfortunately, this is not so. The timeless character of the model is more consonant with an uncertain or even infinite investment horizon paralleling the indefinitely long lives of individual financial assets. There is nothing here which provides a basis for a liquidation date. Let us now turn to considerations of the modifications of the model necessary to make possible an analysis of both hedging and speculative behavior as well.

3. Hedging and Interest Rate Risk

In much of the literature on the term structure hedging behavior is taken as the principal model of institutional portfolio behavior. [24]

---

[23] The slope reflect the intensity of risk aversion among market participants. The more rapidly expected yield rises for a given increment in risk—the smaller the angle between the horizontal axis and the efficient opportunity set in Fig. 3-4—the more intense the aversion to risk. This model takes this intensity as given as well as the amount and kinds of risk to be borne.

[24] This is stressed below and evidence cited in Chapter 4.

Financial intermediaries adopt this strategy as a way to completely eliminate interest rate risk. This policy objective varies sharply from the one represented by the indifference curve tangent at x in Fig. 3-4. The policy depicted there provides for an acceptance of risk (here, of course, default risk) when accompanied by an appropriate return. I have already argued that hedging can eliminate risk only for those with a definite investment horizon such as retiring household.[25] We may ask, then, whether it is possible to incorporate the hedging strategy for this special case in the Sharpe model of portfolio choice. Put somewhat differently, can the hedging strategy be depicted by the set of indifference curves one of which intercepts the expected yield axis of Fig. 3-4 at r_p, the riskless interest rate?

For the corner solution to work the term to maturity of the default-free bonds which are to provide the yield r_p must correspond exactly to the investment horizon at the end of which they are to be liquidated. But, as we have just seen, the Sharpe model has no determinate investment horizon. Let us assign a horizon to the model. Assume that for the moment the period so spanned corresponds to a particular hedger's needs. The situation depicted in Fig. 3-4 by this corner solution might then apply to this special case since there is no risk (no default risk) associated with it. But if other hedgers have other investment horizons, the homogeneity assumption is violated since the opportunity set differs among market participants.[26] Further, even if all hedgers had the same horizon, how are we to treat the risk that would for them be attached to default-free bonds with different maturities? Could the risk and return characteristics of securities with a variety of maturities be plotted on in Fig. 3-4 when a single horizon for other securities has been arbitrarily defined?

That these questions arise suggests that the actuarial analogy by means of which uncertainty is reduced to or made equivalent to certainty is too fragile to bear the weight placed on it. Such a reduction

---

[25] But even here a problem arises if households plan to provide for their descendants. In this event, household could also have indefinitely long lives.

[26] See R. Roll [55] for a discussion of this problem. Roll attempts to include in a simple model both default risk and interest rate risk. He commits himself to the hedging model of portfolio management as evidenced by his use of the horizon period—"the length of time an investor plans to forego consumption and remain invested." His procedure was to do, roughly, what has just been proposed; namely, to assume a horizon to define the riskless maturity. He finds that "individual horizons may vary and a different set of testable equations is necessary for every choice of the market's horizon." His results were "inconclusive with respect to measurement of a unique horizon period applicable to all investors." The argument presented here that interest rate risk arises from disturbances to the opportunity set is consistent with Roll's failure to find a unique horizon since it explicitly rejects the need for one.

begs the question (or these questions). Uncertainty must mean in this context, and this point is central to the main line of reasoning advanced in this book, that yields on all financial assets, default free and risky, are subject to unanticipated change. In the terms of Fig. 3-4, this means that the entire opportunity set may shift so that interest rate risk cannot be depicted in an equilibrium model. More generally, uncertainty must mean nonstationarity in the basic data on which the actuarial matrix is based.

Changes in the data underlying the actuarial matrix can take a number of forms.[27] Alterations can occur in one or more entries in the matrix reflecting changes in the prospects for one or more enterprises. Old enterprises can disappear and new ones can appear causing old entries to disappear and new ones to appear. For the purpose of making clear the disequilibrating character of these changes, let us continue to assume that data collection and processing remain costless but that changes in the data cannot be predicted. We may conclude that the shifts in the opportunity set produced by changes in the data arising from any source will shift the intercept of the boundary and may change its slope as well as alter the relative positions of interior points. The risk posed by the possibility of changes in the intercept of the efficient set is interest rate risk—in terms of the macro-economic models discussed in Chapters 1 and 2, it is the risk that "the interest rate" may change in unanticipated ways.[28]

It might appear that the best way to analyze disturbances to equilibrium is to develop a dynamic model in which the impact of particular disturbance can be specified with mathematical precision. To use static equilibrium models as the primary analytical device to point to the difficulties disequilibrating disturbances produce for portfolio managers can at most give an intuitive feel for what is involved. Thus, it seems rather a loose way to proceed to let the intercept of the efficient set be "the interest rate" and to then assert that there are no supply and demand schedules for loanable funds, but only markets for myriad particular uses of funds none of which is riskless. However, if it were possible, it would be very difficult to develop a model which shows the complex interrelationships between all financial assets and how even a change affecting the prospects of a single

[27]Some mention should be made of the state-preference approach to portfolio choice. See Myers [51] and references cited therein for a discussion which parallels this one. For all their ingenuity those who have developed this approach assume stationarity. Consequently, this work is of little help here.

[28]Following the analysis developed in Chapter 1, since successive one-period rates may change in anticipated ways, successive term structures may also change in anticipated ways. This kind of change is to be sharply distinguished from the shift in observed term structures due to disturbances.

enterprise affects all other financial assets because of these interrelationships. That no such dynamic model exists suggest the limitations of the assumption that information is a free good. Moreover, such rigor, even if achievable, would divert us from our purpose which is to work out the implications of the behavior of the private financial sector for stabilization policy regarding maturity composition of the federal debt. As I shall argue in the next section, it is the impossibility of devising such a dynamic model which is the chief reason for the existence of financial intermediaries.

What does this line of reasoning imply for the traditional distinction between default risk and interest rate risk? It suggests that it is misleading to classify financial assets either as subject to default risk or as riskless. All financial assets are subject to interest rate risk and some are subject to the risk of default as well. It also suggests that it is the uncertainty arising from the nonstationarity of the system that is central to portfolio strategies, both hedging and speculative. The risk of default is just an added complication in the development of strategies to cope with nonstationarity. Moreover, it implies that hedging as traditionally viewed is a pointless strategy for managers of portfolios with indefinite investment horizons since it cannot eliminate interest rate risk. Since such portfolios have no liquidation dates, they will usually contain default-free assets maturing at fixed dates, maturing assets being replaced by new ones as time passes. Unforeseen rises in rates produce windfall decreases in the prices of outstanding unmatured securities, unforeseen declines in rates produce windfall increases in their prices. Only by successful forecasting of these windfalls can losses be fully averted and gains fully captured. Hedging as a strategy excludes forecasting.

Successful forecasting is more complicated than the analysis so far suggests, since U.S. Government securities, which are generally taken to be the empirical counterpart of the theoretically default-free securities, are subject to more than interest rate risk. Most conspicuous is the risk of depreciation in purchasing power stemming from unanticipated inflation.[29] In addition, they are not completely free of default risk since their collateral is not perfect. The collateral behind the contractual payments made by the government is the power to tax. The certainty of these payments depends on the continuity of this power. The probability of revolution is no doubt quite low, and the probability of nuclear war perhaps quite low also. We will proceed as if the continuity of government is certain. We

---

[29] If inflation is fully anticipated, nominal rates will be higher than they otherwise would be, reflecting the rate of increase in the price level.

will not make a similar assumption about the government's ability to maintain a stable price level.[30]

Having identified interest rate risk as resulting from the possibility of disequilibria in the market for financial assets, it remains to be shown what impact the existence of this risk has on the term structure of rates. In Chapter 1, the yield curve simply reflected the known course of one-period rates in the future, sloping upward if one-period rates move up over time, sloping downward if they move down and level if one-period rates remain constant. There are at least two kinds of impact to be considered. First, how do disturbances affect portfolio managers' estimates of the course of rates? There is no reason why different kinds of disturbances should all affect the yield curve in the same way. Put differently, disturbance need not alter successive one-period rates by the same amount or even in the same direction. Second, and more important, what is the relationship between term to maturity and interest rate risk? To answer these questions it will be necessary to consider ways in which the variables listed at the end of Chapter 2 are related to interest rate risk. I shall argue that the magnitude of the risk rises as term to maturity increases because of the way in which shifts in the underlying determining variables affect the course of interest rates.

In Chapter 1, the course of one-period rates was conceived as arising as an equilibrium path which cleared the loanable funds markets in successive periods. For the moment let us keep the assumption that information is costless but that disturbances are unpredictable. We may then turn our attention to how changes in the underlying variables affect these equilibrium rates, or better, shift the equilibrium levels in the successive periods. It is convenient for us to treat these market clearing rates as one-period or short-term rates but it should be recognized that in any given period funds may be borrowed and lent for more than a single period.[31] Let these rates represent the intercept of the corresponding efficient sets in which all expected yield span one period as well as do the actuarial matrixes. We may then pose the question about the timing of the impact of disturbances as follows: how do changes in the underlying variables affect the entries in the successive actuarial matrixes?

---

[30] The problems produced by inflation, anticipated and unanticipated, will not be central to what follows. Even so, it is important to make the distinction between these two situations and not ignore their impact.

[31] There is no easy way to deal with this problem. However, the complications introduced by the recognition that a structure of rates by maturity as well as by default risk is required for each period are not essential to gaining an understanding of the impact of nonstationarity.

The aggregate supply and demand schedules (which, it will be recalled, have no existence independent of the individual uses of funds) reflect the variables which determine productivity and thrift. These variables—technology, demographic characteristics, population and taxes—were taken as given in Chapter 1. In Chapter 2 policy variables were added—government expenditure, taxes, money stock and even the maturity composition of the federal debt.[32] Shifts in any of the variables can cause changes in the entries in some or all of the successive actuarial matrixes and, hence, in the equilibrium levels of the successive one-period rates. The effects of such shifts need not be limited to shifts in intercepts of the efficient set. They can change its shape and the relative position of interior points as well. The difficulties involved in spelling out the complex possibilities have already been noted. We may confine ourselves to exploring possible patterns of change in successive equilibrium levels.

Some examples may help to illustrate the possibilities. Consider first a technological breakthrough such as the development of an inexpensive method of desalinization. For a large number of firms, the marginal efficiency of capital schedules for many successive periods will shift to right in anticipation of the development of desert areas. There may be some firms, say those involved in finding subterranean water sources, whose prospects will be adversely affected. But in the aggregate, successive demand schedules for fund shift relative to supply shifting the new equilibrium one-period rates to higher levels.

Consider next an imposition of a one-period surtax on income by the federal government. Households may reduce current savings to maintain consumption, knowing that they can restore savings in future periods after the surtax is removed. This would shift the aggregate savings schedule to the left in the current period, raising the current one-period rate, and shift the aggregate savings schedules to the right for successive future periods, lowering the corresponding one-period rates in future periods. A change in the tax rate would, of course, have an effect on the course of one-period rates different from the technological change just described.

These examples are but two from a large number which come to mind. The passage of time generously provides new ones. What is central is that the time pattern of changes in one-period rates stemming from shifts in the underlying variables that determine interest rates cannot be deduced from the logic of equilibrium analysis. The

---

[32] Clearly, other policy variables such as the discount rate are important. This is not the place, however, to enter the current controversy on monetary policy. The behavior of the money stock is important, too.

wide variety of possible patterns depend on complex empirical circumstances that can only be fully understood by careful and continuous study. However, some generalizations about these circumstances can be made—and these are corroborated by evidence
presented below[33]—which suggest that shifts in the equilibrium levels
of successive one-period rates tend to be strongly and positively correlated. This positive correlation provides the basic positive relationship I propose between interest rate risk and term to maturity.

We turn now to a consideration of the windfall price changes
caused by disturbances to equilibrium. It is important to distinguish
between the effect of a shift in the equilibrium level of rates and a
shift in the distribution of returns to a particular enterprise. Recalling the desalinization example, a shift in the demand in the output of
a firm will lead to an increase in its returns, at least until the industry
expands its output.[34] The initial impact will be to increase the distribution of returns accruing to the firm's securities, and at the initial
level of rates, this would increase their market value. These same
prospects of increased returns will, as we have seen, lead to a rightward in aggregate demand for loanable funds schedules and raise
rates. For some firms, the effect of the increase in their prospective
returns will offset the effect of the increase level of rates and lead to
an increase in the market value of their securities. For other firms
the reverse will be true. The possibilities of ways the net impact on
market value is distributed among financial assets need not detain us
here. But it is important to recognize that, whatever the direction of
price change between the two equilibria, the interest rate effect
works in the same direction for all assets.

Consider now the relation of the interest rate effect and term to
maturity. To help isolate this relationship we shall focus on debt securities since for them, contractual arrangements exclude debt holders from the windfalls arising from shifts in the distribution of returns.[35] Following the argument as developed in Chapter 1 we may
relate the yield to maturity on debt instruments to successive one-
period rates as follows:

$$(3\text{-}6) \quad 1 + R_{n,t} = [(1 + r_{1,t,t})(1 + r_{1,t,t+1}) \ldots (1 + r_{1,t,t+n-1})]^{1/n}$$

Taken as it stands, this means that the price of such a bond depends

[33] See the discussions on the intercorrelations of times series of government
security price changes in Chapter 4.

[34] These will be short-run and long-run effects and these will depend on industry structure. We need not be concerned with these matters in detail.

[35] However, to the extent that improvements in the prospects of a firm
diminish the default risk of its debt, they improve the position of their debts
holders.

only on the expected course of rates. For the moment let us interpret Eq. 3-6 rather loosely as showing the relationship between expectational elements and observed yields to maturity and leaving quite open the possibility of other influences on yield to maturity.

The impact on the price of a bond of changes in the one-period rates depends on how these rates move in response to disturbances. Let us assume first that movements in rates are perfectly correlated. Disturbances then would produce greater windfall price changes the longer the term to maturity, since the greater would be the number of rates which changed in the same direction. As long as the changes in one-period rates are positively associated, the positive relationships between the magnitude of windfall price changes and term to maturity will persist. If the association between changes in rates were not positive but, say, random, windfall price changes would be independent of term to maturity.

Even though I have argued that the positive association between interest rate risk and term to maturity is rooted in real phenomena, it may still seem to depend chiefly on the contractual characteristic of debt. It may help to amplify matters further to avoid possible confusion on this point. The fundamental source of interest rate risk is the immobility of physical capital.[36] Our highly productive modern technology requires extensive investment in long-lived plant and equipment. A very considerable proportion of this physical capital, once in place, cannot easily be used for purposes other than those for which it was initially designed. Were it costless to convert physical capital to alternative uses, matters would be very different.

The literature on capital budgeting tells us that an appropriate discount rate must be used to make decisions about putting physical capital in place. In terms of the foregoing argument, the yield to maturity spanning the useful life of the equipment is, to a first approximation, the appropriate rate to be used. Since that life is the span of time, the capital is "immobilized."[37] Perhaps even more important is that the useful life of physical capital may not be exogenous but is itself determined with reference to the level of rates as managers de-

[36] Some further comment on the notion of immobility seems desirable. Consider its opposite fluidity. Perfectly fluid capital apart from money cannot serve as a store of services, because the service potential of physical capital inheres in its physical characteristics. Flexibility is possible but some limitations are inevitable if the capital is to be of any use at all. It is the limitations on flow of services from the capital stock which gives rise to immobility.

[37] As is to be expected, there are many complications. For example, adjustments must be made for default risk. Presumably this could be solved by picking the rate from the appropriate location as an interior point in the opportunity set rather than focusing in the riskless rate of interest. We can ignore other complications.

cide the length of time to commit their funds. Let us assume that the capital budgeting decision follows the usual maximization rules, that is, the process is rational and leads to a particular investment being undertaken.[38] Let us assume further that throughout its life the project produces the payoffs that were initially forecast. But also assume that fairly early, the level of rates rose as a consequence of, say, the desalinization breakthrough mentioned earlier. Were the capital in the project in question completely fluid, it would pay to change plans, perhaps converting it in part to new uses and in part changing the techniques used in the project. However, because this capital is immobile this cannot be done.

Interest rate risk, then, arises because of the necessity of making commitments which may turn out to be inappropriate not because of changes in circumstances internal to the enterprise but because of such changes elsewhere. One way to put this is that every productive activity is subject to two classes of risk. The returns to the activity are subject to default risk; that is, the expected returns will not be realized. And often overlooked, the activity itself, because of inflexibilities, is subject to the risk that even if expected returns are realized it may become less valuable in relation to other activities; that is, the opportunity cost may increase.

Borrowers can issue long-term debt and thereby shift this latter burden to some extent to lenders. Lenders can limit the amount of this burden by lending short term.[39] But what about the government debt? As we have already noted, the collateral behind Treasury issues is not productive physical assets though many are available but rather the taxing power of the federal government. The maturity composition of the government is determined through the political process for reasons other than the utility maximization of the kind suggested above whereby borrowers and lenders shift or bear interest rate risk according to the terms of the debt contract.

Even though government debt does not subject its holders to default risk, it subjects them to the same risk of relative deterioration of price due to increases in opportunity costs that private debt does. It is as though the government can create by fiat immobile physical capital with arbitrarily variable useful life spans. If portfolio managers are averse to this opportunity cost or interest rate risk as well as

---

[38] Rationality as the maximization of present value makes sense in a stationary context such as Sharpe's in which uncertainty is reduced to a special kind of certainty. When expectations diverge and disturbances are possible it is not always clear what action maximizes present values.

[39] While some risk can be shifted in this way, all of it cannot since the enterprise cannot be entirely financed by debt. At the other extreme, call money provides lenders with a means to avoid interest rate risk entirely.

to default risk—and there seems to be no reason why the risk of an unfavorable outcome caused by a change in the data should be more desirable than the risk of an unfavorable outcome arising from a given set of data—the maturity composition of the government debt will influence the level and structure of interest rates and through this influence the level of economic activity.

The links between changes in maturity composition and economic activity are these. Because interest rate risk is undesirable, the prices of dated securities are lower than they would otherwise be in proportion to the amount of time they span, given the levels of successive short-period rates. The price of perpetuities are similarly affected. Yields to maturity are consequently higher by an amount which we may designate a term premium, term premiums being an increasing function of term to maturity. The magnitude and rate of increase in term premiums depends on, among other things, the amount of interest rate risk to be borne. Alterations of the maturity composition changes the amount of interest rate risk in the system, increases in average maturity increasing the magnitude of term premiums, and decreases in average maturity decreasing them. Investment and consumption expenditure decisions depend on the level and structure of interest rates. Term premiums are a component part of expected yields on financial assets so that changes in them affect these expenditures. For example, an increase in term premiums will lead, other things equal, to a decrease in investment expenditures. The argument holds for the relationship of interest rates to price level changes and to the balance of payments.[40]

Because this explanation of the term structure differs in significant ways from the theories of the term structure reviewed below, it will be helpful to distinguish it rather sharply from the others. To do this we may call it the term premium hypothesis, where term premiums are defined as the difference between the yields to maturity as given in (3-6) and what they are observed to be. Thus,

$$(3\text{-}7) \qquad\qquad T_{n,t} = R^0_{n,t} - R_{n,t}$$

where $R^0_{n,t}$ is observed. Unfortunately, $R_{n,t}$ cannot be observed directly. The hypothesis states that $T = T(M, U)$, M being an index measuring the extent of interest rate risk, and U the utility functions of market participants. Utility functions are such that $\partial T/\partial M > 0$.

Two points remain to be made about the analysis leading to the term premium hypothesis. First, we have retained the assumption

---

[40] To the extent that increases in domestic short-term rates relative to such rates elsewhere attract and keep "hot" money, increases in maturity composition will reduce capital outflows. We return to this matter below in Chapter 7.

that information is a free good, that while disturbances are unpredictable, once they have occurred, adjustments to them are instantaneous. This may seem a bit strained but it is quite common to adopt this line of reasoning in discussions of term structure. The assumption could be neutral but it is not; it creates an implied bias toward stationarity. This brings us to the second point.

This bias toward stationarity or, better, toward obscuring nonstationarity, can be seen in the term premium function which rationalizes Eq. 3-7. As it stands it is easy to regard the function T as a stable one, but it is not legitimate to do so. The Sharpe model using the homogeneity of expectations assumption implied stationarity, but I have argued that interest rate risk arises out of nonstationarity. Might not keeping the homogeneity assumption essentially intact lead us to believe that there is some higher level stationary process which generates disturbances that create interest rate risk but which would make the T function stable? There is no reason to suppose that this is so. Yet this is implicit in most term structure hypotheses.

The T function given above might best be regarded as descriptive of certain characteristics of a higher level process that cannot be regarded as stationary in any ordinary sense. I offer no theories here of how the entries in the actuarial matrix appear, disappear or change. My preference is to leave the question open. However, in the absence of a strong showing of stationarity at a higher level, any analysis of uncertainty must confront the problem of nonstationarity directly rather than ignoring it by analyzing stationary problems like default risk. This suggests it is time to relax the homogeneity of expectations assumption and take account of the costs of collecting and processing information.

4. Subjective Risk and Speculative Behavior

What are the implications of this higher level nonstationarity for portfolio management? Clearly, the model of portfolio management as once for all and costless selection from a stable opportunity set can at most be a point of departure for understanding what is involved in portfolio management under uncertainty. For a full understanding, portfolio management must be seen as a system of continuous management capable of generating portfolio strategies to cope with this nonstationarity. Furthermore, this system will reflect the fact that information is not a free good, that it takes time and other resources to collect and process it and that the passage of time can bring changes in the data which invalidate previously established forecasts of risk and returns on available opportunities.

An important consequence of the recognition that information processing is costly is that the homogeneity of expectations can no longer be assumed. However, even if portfolio managers need not assume that other managers do not share their views they need not recognize that divergent views exist. Heterogeneous expectations could thus imply no more than a different opportunity set of the kind depicted in Fig. 3-3 for each manager. If we go no further than this, portfolio management is still confined to a once for all selection. However, if managers recognize that differences in expectations exist, that they exist because of possibility of changes in basic data, and that it is possible to ferret out and process information that can be used to forecast such changes, the possibility of speculative strategies arises. Changes in the basic data produce windfall security price changes. For those who can develop effective forecasting techniques, speculative gains are to be had by capturing windfall increases and avoiding windfall decreases.

It is the prospect of speculative gains, not just once for all but on a continuing basis that provides the incentive for the collection and processing of information essential for security price to reflect opportunity costs. If there is no possibility of gain, there would be no possibility of individual actuarial matrixes, not to mention a common one for all market participants, since the fundamental nonstationarity of the system would make security prices a chaotic jumble. This incentive to process information imparts to security markets a tendency to order and structure which many writers take as given. It is my contention that the structures, or better, tendencies toward structure, in security markets can only be understood through a model of portfolio management which gives a central role to speculative strategies.

Having asserted the importance of such a model, some description of what is involved in successful speculation is in order. Evidence supporting the assertion is even more desirable, but we shall turn to that below. An effective portfolio management system of the kind proposed here will have at least the following four elements. First it must have the capacity to generate actuarial matrixes on a continuous basis. This means systematic search for information bearing on prospective changes in the basic data and timely incorporation of new information into the body of previously accumulated information. Second, it must provide a means of determining the extent to which it produces results different from systems employed by other portfolio managers. Put differently, this means it must have the capacity to generate, in addition to its own opportunity set, the opportunity set as seen by the "market." Third, it must provide a means by which to identify significant discrepancies between its own and other or market views of investment opportunities. Finally, it must facilitate the development and mounting of plans of action or strategies to exploit discrepancies so identified. Perhaps an example will help to give body to this description.

Suppose a portfolio manager has projected on the basis of newly acquired information[41] a fairly active demand for loanable funds over the next five to ten years after having previously viewed these prospects less favorably. Suppose further that he judges the "market," that is, most other lenders, to share the views he previously held, namely, that demand for funds would not be brisk. He might conclude that the course of interest rate would be higher over the next ten years than most people expected. If so, what action should he take?

If he is confident of his judgment, he will believe that others will come to share his views. When this occurs, longer-term rates will rise producing windfall price decline on longer-term issues. He will reduce the average maturity of his portfolio, the extent of this shift depending on, among other things, the extent of the confidence he has in his own judgment. This shift can be made by selling currently held assets, and by the investment of cash generated by maturing assets.

But this is not all. Since he has made a judgment about future events—namely, that the information he has will eventually become available and lead others to the conclusions he has reached—he should be able to specify a probable time interval at the end of which the forecasts of others will be revised. By careful monitoring he can determine whether his initial projection was correct or in error. If others do not come to share his view, security prices will not fall. This failure is itself valuable information on the efficiency of the forecasting techniques employed, and can, perhaps, be used to improve forecasting accuracy. More importantly, the portfolio will be adjusted to reflect the best course of action in the light of the actual outcome. In the case of failure of rates to rise as forecasted, the appropriate response may be to restore the maturity composition to what it was before this plan of action was adopted. Appropriateness will depend, however, not only on the relationship between forecasted and realized outcomes but on current forecasts as well.

Taking a speculative position, whether to lengthen or shorten average maturity, depends on the portfolio manager's confidence that his forecast differs significantly from the market's. What determines maturity composition—we confine ourselves to this simple dimension for simplicity of exposition—when the manager agrees with the market? Alternatively, what position is to be taken when disturbances

---

[41] For example, he may have learned about the desalinization breakthrough.

must be regarded as unpredictable? It must be emphasized that spec-ulative opportunities need not always be available. Some policy must be adopted to serve as the basis from which speculative departures are made. The matching of asset and liability maturities, for example long-term bonds for life insurance companies, is one such policy. But I have argued at some length that matching or hedging cannot eliminate or even reduce interest rate risk. Further, even the charac-terization of policy by means of indifference curves can be mislead-ing since this procedure sometimes implicitly and often explicitly takes for granted a stationary environment.

In Chapter 6 a theory of how institutions decide policy is pro-posed as an alternative to the widely used hedging model of institu-tional portfolio behavior. The theory posits an institutional utility function that governs the level of interest rate risk to be borne for both speculative and nonspeculative situations. These policies reflect the attitudes of the managers and what are often referred to as "insti-tutional" considerations. These later factors are often regarded as irrational; that is, that because of them, institutions follow policies which reduce profits. I shall argue later that it is not necessary to ex-plain institutional portfolio behavior in this way. I shall argue instead that institutions can be regarded as adopting a pattern of continuous coping with nonstationarity motivated by the prospect of gain suffi-cient to offset the cost of collecting and processing information and conditioned by their own experience of the historical record of shifts in the underlying variables that determine the level of interest rates and by the "institutional" characteristics of their financial industry.[42]

For the present we may characterize the base policy that governs maturity composition when no speculative position in opposition to the market can be justified as extrapolative. Portfolio managers under these ordinary or base conditions extrapolate past trends in rates from past and current term structures to make a forecast of the future course of interest rates.[43] Such data is publicly available and

---

[42] By institutional characteristics is meant the expectations and understand-ings that have developed among depositors, stockholders, insurance purchasers from the past performance of financial institutions. Moreover, practice is pre-sumably not arbitrarily determined initially. This will be considered more fully in Chapter 6.

[43] Some mention should be made of the problem portfolio managers might have in determining what the "market" expectations of the course of interest rates is. If the matter was as given in Chapter 1, forward rates which are observ-able could be taken as unbiased estimates of future one-period rates. Forward rates become quite ambiguous once term premiums are taken into account since these make yields to maturity, and hence forward rates, greater than they other-wise would be. To unscramble observed term structures portfolio managers must have a procedure for estimating term premiums. At best, this makes extrapola-tion a probabilistic process; at worst, very complicated indeed. We will return to these complications below in Chapter 5.

can offer no special advantage to particular managers. Extrapolation, thus, does not involve independent assessments of successive supply and demand schedules in future periods of the kind involved in speculative strategies. At any point in time, institutional factors together with the historical record and the current term structure will lead to a base maturity composition. An extrapolative policy then seeks not to avoid interest rate risk as a hedging policy purports to do, but rather aims at finding an acceptable trade-off between this risk and return. Finally, since the trade-offs cannot be taken as constant, an extrapolative policy entails continuous review and adjustment in the light of unfolding events.

Portfolio managers may both speculate and extrapolate: they need not be confined as in the hedger-speculator dichotomy to only one kind of behavior. Not only may managers alternate portfolio strategies over time but may engage in both at the same time. Consider that the range of assets that can be included in a portfolio is very large and information about many of the opportunities very costly or even nonexistent. Institutions do specialize in a limited range of assets estimating default risk in particular areas such as home mortgages or commercial loans to particular industries. Portfolio managers may also specialize in forecasting certain kind of disturbances by focusing on particular attention to government policy and others specialize in developments in other underlying variables, say those which affect the demand for residential housing. Consequently, they may take an extrapolative position with respect to some underlying variables and speculate with respect to others.

Thus, not only under subjective risk do different managers see the opportunity set differently, but opportunity sets contain different subsets of the total opportunities available. Moreover, the total number of opportunities is itself subject to change. Managers know these gaps exist and that their own estimates of investment opportunities can and do differ from those held by others and that all this is subject to change. The prospects of speculative profits is the incentive which leads the managers to undertake the information processing which imparts a tendency toward order in what would otherwise be a chaotic jumble of security prices. What then does this interpretation mean for observed term structures and for policy regarding the maturity composition of the government debt?

To answer this question we may summarize the preceding argument as follows:

1. At a given point in time the term structure will not reflect homogeneous expectations of the course of interest rates as it would if information was a free good and departures from equilibrium were not possible. Expectations will, in the general case, diverge. Differ-

ent participants will focus on different sets of data and process the data differently. Some will be speculating, others extrapolating.

2. The passage of time brings with it both learning and disruption. Managers discover forecast errors as events unfold and use them to revise existing forecasts as well as to improve forecasting techniques. If sufficient time passed without shifts in the underlying variables, learning would produce a consensus about the course of rates because erroneous projections could be corrected. Shifts in real variables disrupt this learning process. The prospect of gains from successful forecasting of such disruption together with the learning opportunities offered by the passage of time impart to security a tendency toward order—relevant information is brought to bear and influences the prices at which transactions occur.

3. The tendency toward equilibrium means that at any given point in time the term structure of interest rates reflects something of a consensus about the course of rates. The yields to maturity, however, contain a term premium which is greater, the greater the amount of time the yield in question spans. This result arises because interest rate risk in a security increases as the amount of time spanned to its maturity increases. The relationship is rooted in the relative immobility of physical capital and is not a financial epiphenomenon. This result also depends on widespread aversion to interest rate risk.

4. Stabilization authorities can affect the structure and level of interest rates by altering the maturity composition of the government debt. Given interest rate risk and aversion to it, variation in maturity composition affords the government a power alien to being able to arbitrarily change the life span of physical capital and the contractual commitment associated with it.

In the following chapters the available evidence will be brought to bear on this interpretation. Unfortunately, it will not be easy to reach firm conclusions about it. One reason is that the term premium hypothesis advanced here is rather complicated as hypotheses in this area go, and direct tests of simple hypotheses have been hard to achieve. Moreover, nearly all the work that has been done in the area of testing term structure hypotheses use the hedger-speculator dichotomy as a model of institutional portfolio behavior. This has colored the interpretations given the results but has also affected the way tests have been constructed and data collected. Let us now turn to this work. Because the more conventional notion of the risk associated with default-free securities has limited the applicability of this work in important ways, a brief statement of the concept of interest rate risk offered here as an alternative may help us to focus more sharply on what is needed to go beyond these limitations.

The aggregate models presented in the first two chapters provided a basis for classifying the determinants of the term structure of interest rates; namely productivity, thrift, and government policy were seen as the factors influencing the interest rates which clear successive markets for loanable funds, given population, technology, and tastes. Because the factors taken as given are in fact subject to disturbance, a risk arises. These disturbances are not to be regarded as normal "noise" or variation that may occur in a stationary system, but rather as evidence of the nonstationarity of the system. This nonstationarity produces untoward consequences in a world in which long-lived capital is not perfectly fluid. This immobility means that the consequences of nonstationarity cannot be eliminated, though they may be mitigated.

It is the risk associated with this partly manageable, but irreducible aspect of the consequence of nonstationarity that I have termed interest rate risk. Conceived in this way, interest rate risk is not something which can be avoided but which must be confronted. I shall argue below that much of what goes on in financial intermedies can be understood as coping with an unavoidable interest rate risk.

chapter 4

The Term Structure of Interest Rates: Theories and Evidence

The term premium hypothesis advanced in Chapter 3 is but one of a number of alternative explanations of the term structure of interest rates and one which has not had wide currency. Most of the alternative hypotheses depend crucially on the hedger-speculator dichotomy to characterize portfolio management and this dependence has strongly influenced the choice of data and the interpretation of the findings of empirical work designed to test these hypotheses. Consequently, in reviewing these findings to determine the extent to which they support or contradict the term premium hypothesis, it will be necessary to review carefully the various alternative hypotheses to determine the extent to which data collected and organized to test them can be brought to bear on a rather different hypothesis. Perhaps of equal or even greater importance would be an overview of the literature on the term structure.

We begin our review with a consideration of three relatively simple static equilibrium hypotheses. In the next chapter we will take up some of the complications neglected here. At one pole is the traditional expectations hypothesis which holds that yields to maturity depend entirely on the expected course of successive short-period rates as represented in Eq. 3-6. In effect, uncertainty about the course of future rates has no effect on the structure of rates. More toward the center of this spectrum of views is the liquidity preference hypothesis, which holds that widespread risk aversion influences the rate structure as well as expectations about the course of rates, though, as we shall see, uncertainty is conceived very differently here from the account given in the preceding chapter. At the other pole is the segmented market hypothesis which asserts that expectations have little or no effect on the term structure because the market for securities of differing maturities is segmented: that is, portfolio managers regard securities of different maturities as very imperfect substitutes at best. As a consequence, prices of securities are determined by factors internal to each of the separate markets.

Each hypothesis relies on the hedger-speculator dichotomy for its theory of portfolio management, the differences between them turning on the relative weights given to hedgers and speculators and the attitude toward risk assigned to speculators. Before turning to the empirical work bearing on these hypotheses, it will be useful to spell out in some detail the way in which the hypotheses depend on this dichotomy, especially since the latter has been subjected to such extensive criticism above.

A particularly succinct statement of the hedger-speculator dichotomy as a portfolio management theory is that advanced by Modigliani and Sutch [50]. Following their argument, market participants have preferred maturity habitats which reflect the desire, and serve to eliminate interest rate risk by insuring that maturing assets provide sufficient cash to meet liabilities as they fall due. The time path of maturing liabilities is known with certainty. Preferred habitats will vary; banks will have short ones, insurance companies long ones. Departures from the preferred habitat can be of two kinds, both of which, they argue, lead to the failure of assets to absorb, as it were, the potential risk maturing liabilities pose. Thus, if assets are "too long," losses may ensue when assets are sold prior to maturity because of unanticipated increases in interest rates.[1] Conversely, if assets are "too short," income may diminish because of unanticipated decreases in rates. Diminished income when left to accumulate to meet liabilities coming due later will not grow to the amount previously expected. But when assets are in the preferred habitat, the portfolio manager "will know exactly the outcome of his investment as measured by the terminal value of his wealth." This is of course the hedging rationale criticized in Chapter 3. Because in the segmented markets hypothesis this rationale is held to be the predominant guide to portfolio management, it will be helpful to explore it more fully in the context of this hypothesis before turning to the empirical work.

In the segmented market hypothesis, the influence of liability

---

[1] There has been some confusion about when such losses actually occur. For example, as long as windfall losses of this kind are merely "paper losses"—that is, as long as the assets are not sold—they are not real. This line of reasoning has been advanced to explain why banks cannot sell long-term governments during booms. See Chase [10] for a discussion of the "lock-in" effect. Apart from tax considerations, which are not negligible, paper losses are real and occur when the market price declines.

characteristics will lead portfolio managers to keep to their habitats without regard to expectations about the course of rates. Indeed, "speculation in debt markets will be primarily based upon short planning periods" [13, p. 497]; and so will exert very little, if any, influence on the term structure. While there may be portfolio managers who speculate, their impact on prices can be safely disregarded. Now, as we have seen, hedgers need not forecast interest rates, though they may forecast outlay streams. Moreover, since forecasting interest rates is costly and the benefits to them will be nil, and since they do not need them to achieve their preferred habitat, they will not forecast. The term structure cannot, therefore, be regarded reflecting the course of successive short-period rates.[2]

Why should portfolio mangers behave in this way? It could be argued that the forecasting techniques available to them produce results not sufficiently better than could be obtained by chance alone to permit them to cover their costs so that, perforce, they rely on rules of thumb and habit. While this may be true for some, if it is true for virtually all portfolio managers, the security markets cannot be regarded as even tending to reflect the opportunity costs of investment since there will be no way for new information to affect security prices.[3]   However, if it is possible to make speculative profits by successful forecasting, but no one chooses to do so, we are left with a kind of widespread irrationality. The theory of institutional portfolio management advanced in Chapter 6 provides a means for including institutional preferences without involving irrational behavior. For the moment, then, we can neglect the segmented market hypothesis.

A. THE EXPECTATIONS HYPOTHESIS

The expectations hypothesis has a long history but the main empirical work bearing on it dates from David Meiselman's path-break-

---

[2] Tests of such a hypothesis are difficult since almost any relationship between yields in different markets could be rationalized. Thus if the prices of all maturities move up and down together, it could be argued that some nonexpectational factor common to all markets was at work. Perhaps the most satisfying position is that price movements in different markets should be unrelated. See, J. Michaelsen [44] for a discussion of one such test.

[3] The cost of undertaking investment is foregone benefits of consumption. The interest rate measures this cost by showing the trade-off between future and current consumption. If market prices, and hence yield to maturity, are determined without regard to future and present supply and demand schedules for loanable funds, they cannot bear any systematic relationship to this fundamental trade-off relationship.

ing work on the subject.[4] Meiselman accepts the hedger-speculator theory of portfolio management, but rather than assigning a dominant role to hedgers who stay in their preferred habitats regardless of opportunities for speculative profits, he argues that hedging behavior has no impact. Thus, Meiselman assumes

> that short and long-term securities can be treated as if they were perfect substitutes and that transactors, indifferent to uncertainty, and having similar expectations, equate the forward rates in the markets to the expected rates. As a matter of descriptive reality, individual transactors may still speculate or hedge on the basis of risk aversion, but the speculators who are indifferent to uncertainty will bulk sufficiently large to determine market rates on the basis of their mathematical expectations alone. [43, p. 10]

This means that Eq. 3-6, repeated here for convenience,

$$(3\text{-}6) \qquad 1 + R_{n,t} = [(1 + r_{1,t,t})(1 + r_{1,t,t+1}) \cdots (1 + r_{1,t,t+n-1})]^{1/n}$$

is to be taken literally. The relationship of yields to maturity to the expected course of one-period rates is formally the same as set forth in the classical model: the introduction of uncertainty has no significant impact. In terms of the analysis set forth in Chapter 3 the $r_{n,t,s}$ represent homogeneous expectations held by the dominant group of speculators who, because of their indifference to risk, ignore the dispersion of possible one-period rates about their equilibrium values.

This hypothesis has the interesting implication that, at any given time, the course of rates can be derived from observed yields to maturity. Define a forward rate as follows:[5]

$$(4\text{-}1) \qquad F_{1,t,+n-1} = \frac{(1 + R_{n,t})^n}{(1 + R_{n-1,t})^{n-1}}$$

Then, for any pair of bonds whose maturities differ by one period, a forward rate can be derived corresponding to the $r_{1,t,s}$ in Eq. 3-6. Meiselman's hypothesis then may be seen to imply that forward rates are unbiased estimates of expected rates; that is,

---

[4] For example, see F. A. Lutz [36] and J. R. Hicks [28]. Early empirical work is that of F. R. Macaulay [37] and B. Hickman [27], the latter as reported in D. Meiselman [43, pp. 11–12].

[5] To illustrate, assume a three-period yield of 5 percent and a two-period yield of 4 percent. The forward one-period rate applicable to period three is

$$\frac{(1.05)^3}{(1.04)^2} - 1 = 0.703$$

or 7.03 percent. The arithmetic becomes somewhat complicated by coupons. For a discussion of these complications, see Meiselman [43, p. 2]. If all bonds are in the form of discounted notes such as Treasury bills, the relationship would hold exactly.

(4-2) $F_{1,t,s} = r_{1,t,s}$ for all s

One way to test this hypothesis is to gather independent evidence from the appropriate group of speculators on what their expectations of the $r_{1,t,s}$ were at time t and compare these to the observed $F_{1,t,s}$. The hypothesis would be shown in error if the $r_{1,t,s}$ and the $F_{1,t,s}$ differed, subject to the usual provisions of sampling error. However, independent evidence is very difficult to come by and what there is suggests diverse, not homogeneous expectations.[6] Consequently, direct tests of the hypothesis appear to be ruled out. Meiselman's major contribution was to provide a very ingenious indirect test. Before turning to Meiselman's empirical work it will be helpful to consider a little more carefully the meaning of speculation in this context.

Recall that, as described in Section B-4 of Chapter 3, opportunities for speculation arose only when a divergence of forecasts of the course of rates arose. A portfolio manager could take a speculative position only when he saw a discrepancy between his views and the market and if he was confident that his judgment was sound. No such discrepancies can arise in Meiselman's world, though as we shall see, discrepancies of a different and very special kind are crucial to it. What Meiselman does is to maintain the fiction of free information and the consequent homogeneity of expectations as was done in the previous chapter up to Section B-4. We saw there that this assumption begged the questions of how and why information was collected and processed. Moreover, if forecasting is costless for some it is hard to see why it is not costless for all, yet Meiselman accepts the existence of a class of nonforecasting hedgers and then rules out their influence on the yield structure. He essentially rules out speculation aimed at profiting from a superior forecasting ability and with it any rationale for the existence of financial intermediaries. An additional consequence of proceeding in this way is to observe the connection between the variables listed at the end of Chapter 2 and the level of the interest rates. As we shall see, expectations of future rates, under these circumstances, quite easily come to depend chiefly on past security prices rather than projections of real and policy variables.

Meiselman developed a special theory of portfolio management for speculators that served in his view to make readily observable times series data into a surrogate for direct observations of expectations at a point in time. The central feature of this special theory was a mechanism by which speculators revised their current forecasts

[6] Survey evidence will be reviewed in Chapter 5. See Kane and Malkiel [31].

on the basis of errors discovered in previous forecasts.[7] It turns out that the tests Meiselman conducted were tests of this error-learning mechanism rather than tests of the expectations hypothesis directly. The mechanism was held to work in the following way. At some previous time, say at the beginning of the previous period, a term structure could be observed that reflected the expected course of one-period rates at that time. By following the computation procedure given in Eq. 4-1 using $R_{1,t-1}$ and $R_{2,t-1}$, the forward rate $F_{1,t-1,t}$ can be derived.[8] This observed rate is, according to the expectations hypothesis, an estimate of the one-period rate, $R_{1,t}$, to rule in period t. When the beginning of period t arrives, $R_{1,t}$ can be observed directly and compared with $F_{1,t-1,t}$, any difference between them being regarded as a forecasting error. Such errors provide the opportunity for learning which takes the form of revision of forecasts of all successive one-period rates applicable at $t + 1$ and after.[9]

Meiselman postulated that the error-learning mechanism would make all such revision a function of the forecast error. Define the error $E_t = R_{1,t} - F_{1,t-1,t}$. Then, in general, the revision, $r_{1,t,t+n} - r_{1,t-1,t+n} = \Delta r_{1,t,t+n}$, depends on the error as follows:

(4-3) $$\Delta r_{1,t,t+n} = e(E_t)$$

In particular, Meiselman assumed the function e to be linear so that

(4-4) $$\Delta r_{1,t,t+n} = a + bE_t + u_t$$

Using annual data from 1901–1954 he estimated Eq. 4-4 and found that changes in forward one-year rates were highly correlated with forecasting errors.[10] The main results are displayed in Table 4-1.

The principal results are three: all regression coefficients are significantly positive; the regression and correlation coefficients decline as time spanned by the equation increases; and the constant terms do not differ significantly from zero. Meiselman interpreted these results, especially the significantly positive regression coefficients, as

---

[7] Meiselman does not discuss how forecasts are initially made. It is as if in the distant past speculators made a forecast based on projection of the underlying variables economic theory specifies as determinants of interest rates and, then, forever after observed errors rather than information on these variables to determine expectations.

[8] See footnote 5 above.

[9] It is important to emphasize that the discrepancies between forecasted and realized one-period rates and learning that Meiselman believes they give rise to are not the same as the discrepancies and learning described in Chapter 3. The latter arise only when expectations diverge; thus, errors will differ among speculators and use they make of them will differ as well. Learning in the latter case is concerned with developing effective systems of information processing "mechanisms" that Meiselman does not consider.

[10] The data were derived from yield curves estimated by Durand [17].

TABLE 4-1

Meiselman's Test of the Error-Learning Mechanism

Regression Results: Equation 4-4

(Units of percentage points)

M (in years)	Constant Term a (and its standard error)	Regression Coefficient b	Correlation Coefficient
1	0.00 (0.02)	0.703	0.952
2	0.00 (0.03)	0.526	0.867
3	-0.01 (0.04)	0.403	0.768
4	-0.03 (0.04)	0.326	0.682
5	-0.02 (0.04)	0.277	0.642
6	-0.01 (0.03)	0.233	0.625
7	-0.02 (0.03)	0.239	0.631
8	0.01 (0.03)	0.208	0.590

supporting his special portfolio management hypothesis and, hence, as supporting indirectly the expectations hypothesis as well. He interpreted the decline in regression and correlation coefficients with time as showing that the forecasts of the more distant future are more firmly held than nearer term forecasts. We shall return to question this interpretation later.[11] The small or zero constant terms were, in his view, of particular significance since if these were different from zero it would mean that forecasts would be revised even when no forecast error occurred and this would be at variance with the error-learning mechanism as he proposed it.

This interpretation of the constant term has been questioned. We shall return to this problem shortly when we turn to the liquidity preference hypothesis. For the present, however, it will be helpful to focus on other aspects of Meiselman's interpretation of his results. First, it must be emphasized that the expectations hypothesis could be true even if the error-learning hypothesis was not. Consequently, the expectations hypothesis could still be true no matter what the result of estimating Eq. 4-4. For example, suppose all regression coefficients, correlation coefficients and constant terms were not different from zero. This would mean that discrepancies between actual and previously implicit one-year rates, that is, forecast errors, are not used to revise contemporaneous forecasts in the manner proposed. It would not mean that forward rates are not unbiased estimates of expected rates.

One way of viewing the expectations hypothesis is to see it as a statement that portfolio managers act rationally. Thus, it is rational to conduct one's affair with regard to what the future holds. A test

[11] Later in this chapter we will have an opportunity to review results from some extensive time series data which call into question Meiselman's error-learning mechanism. See pages 99 and following.

of rational conduct requires two things; a specification of what the future holds that makes it possible to distinguish between rational and irrational behavior in a given context and observation of behavior in that context. In the present context, behavior can be regarded as rational only with reference to the participants' forecasts of the future. The behavior that Meiselman observes—it is behavior inferred from changes in prices not of individual portfolio managers—can be neither rational nor irrational since we do not know what the actors thought the future held. In a word, we need an explicit forecasting hypothesis, not simply one of how forecasts are revised, as well as an hypothesis about what portfolio managers do with their forecasts. We will look at some explicit forecasting hypotheses in Chapter 5.

A second difficulty with Meiselman's interpretation of his findings is that it is not clear how errors can arise. If the speculators who dominate the market always have identical expectations and so act to keep the market in a continuous equilibrium which reflects these expectations, how can price be other than consistent with expectations, since errors can occur only if prices are inconsistent with expectations?

Meiselman's answer is as follows:

> Although the model asserts that forward rates change because of errors made in anticipating the short-term rate, it must be emphasized that the unanticipated change in the short-term rate is only the proximate cause of the revision of expectations. *The real but statistically unspecified independent variable is unanticipated changes in what the literature would typically call "the interest rate."* [43, p. 31]

The solution is something of a *deus ex machina.*[12] In Chapter 3, unanticipated changes in "the interest rate" were discussed at length. It was argued that it was the possibility of speculative gain which led portfolio managers to continuously monitor the flow of information and take positions when conditions appeared favorable. In general, unanticipated changes would never occur unless information about changes in the underlying variables came to the attention of speculators. Yet in Meiselman's model, speculators never are concerned with the underlying variables (except perhaps at some remote initial date) but manage their portfolios entirely on the basis of readily observable changes in security prices.

Futhermore, if expectations are revised in this way it would be necessary to show that the error occurs first and the revision follows after. But with annual data, error and revision can only be regarded as occurring simultaneously. It may, perhaps, be safe to infer that unanticipated shifts in "the interest rate" are, as argued in Chapter 3,

---

[12] This point is developed in Chapter 7 of Terrell [63].

really shifts in the same direction in a considerable number of successive one-period rates and this occurs for empirical, not logical, reasons.[13]   If this be so, there remains little reason to regard the positive correlation of price changes as evidence of an error-learning mechanism.

Finally, two investigators, J. A. G. Grant [25] and A. Buse [8] have argued that the regularities Meiselman found—the significant positive regression coefficient together with declining values in the regression and correlation coefficient as time spawned increases—are spurious. This spuriousness, they argue, is due primarily to the fact that yield curves from which Meiselman obtained his data were produced by a smoothing process. Buse states:

> The Meiselman model is consistent with any set of smoothed yield curves in which the short and long rates move together but in which short rates show greater variability.
> Meiselman-type results may simply be an alternative measure of the economic regularity which shows that short rates have greater variability than long rates and hence do not lend support to any theory of investor behavior. [8, p. 61][14]

B. THE LIQUIDITY PREFERENCE HYPOTHESIS

The theory of portfolio management at the heart of this hypothesis closely resembles the one we have just seen. Portfolio managers are of two kinds, hedgers who stay in their preferred habitat and speculators who are willing to depart from it. It may prove useful to call these latter managers "arbitrageurs" to distinguish them from those who take speculative positions against the market on the basis of forecasts generated by some kind of continuous information processing. These arbitrageurs, then, are willing to depart from their preferred habitats but only for a price that will compensate them for the risk involved for they are averse to risk.[15]   They are most liquid (safe) in their preferred habitat: they will move out of it only if com-

---

[13] These empirical reasons were outlined in Chapter 3.

[14] Meiselman anticipated this criticism to some extent when he constructed a naive model in which short-term and long-term rates tended to move in the same direction as an alternative to his error-learning mechanism. Grant says, however, that "[t]he difficulty of distinguishing between [Meiselman's] error-learning model and the naive model . . . becomes significant when it is realized that the Durand yield curves were even more 'artificial' in construction than yield curves usually are [25, p. 58]."

[15] Arbitrage usually applies to only certain outcomes, ones for which the expected return is the mean of a distribution with zero variance. However, there is ample precedence for this use. For example, Modigliani and Miller [49] make extensive use of it for the case in which the variance is not zero. What is at issue here is whether uncertainty can be reduced to certainty equivalence or whether

pensated by liquidity premiums. Without such compensating differential they prefer to remain liquid.

What is the relationship of these equalizing differentials to expectations? Presumably, illiquidity or risk arises from departure from preferred habitats whether in the direction of lengthening or of shortening asset maturities. The price concessions arbitrageurs require from borrowers for such departures could lead to higher yields on long-term or short-term assets depending on whether departures from frequent habitats were in a lengthening or shortening direction. The most widely accepted view is that there is a "constitutional weakness" in the market which makes price concessions greatest on the longer-term assets. The weakness stems from a predominance of borrowers who wish to borrow long facing lenders who have relatively short preferred habitats.

The mismatch of preferences between lenders and borrowers gives rise to the following relationship between yields to maturity and expected one-period rates:

$$1 + R_{n,t} = [(1 + r_{1,t,t})(1 + r_{1,t,t+1} + L_{1,t,t+1})$$

(4-5)
$$\cdots (1 + r_{1,t,t+n-1} + L_{1,t,t+n-1})]^{1/n}$$

where the $L_{1,t,t+n}$ are liquidity premiums applicable to the corresponding future periods and which, because of the mismatch between borrower and lender preferences already noted, increase as the period to which they are applicable becomes more distant into the future. Comparing this expression to Eq. 3-6 and assuming the $r_{1,t,t+n}$ identical in both situations, the presence of the $L_{1,t,t+n}$ will make yields to maturity under the liquidity preference hypothesis larger than they otherwise would be, the difference increasing as the time spanned by the yield increases.

As a consequence, forward rates will be biased estimates of expected rates, for the computation following Eq. 4-1 will now be

(4-6) $$F_{1,t,t+n-1} = r_{1,t,t+n-1} + L_{1,t,t+n-1}$$

This being so, how do arbitrageurs know that their expectations are the same as the markets as they do under the expectations hypothesis? At any point in time, an infinite number of expected rates and liquidity premiums are consistent with any actual term structure with its set of implicit forward rates. If all arbitrageurs know what the $L_{1,t,t+m}$ are, then of course the situation parallels the simpler one

---

it is irreducible. It can be reduced to certainty only in stationary systems. That the term can be used shows that many analysts have not come to term with uncertainty as an irreducible concomitance on nonstationarity.

given by Eq. 4-2. But if arbitrageurs could know this, then surely scholars should be able to measure liquidity premiums. As we shall see, they have not done so. Moreover, if expectations are not homogeneous, the error-learning mechanism is in serious trouble because the passage of time will produce different errors for different portfolio managers. Consequently, no single set of revisions can be consistent with all of the errors. We shall return to the problems raised by diverse expectations below.

Central to the question of measuring liquidity premiums is the stationarity of the system, or better, the lack of it. Recall that the term premiums, the T_{n_t} of Eq. 3-7, were not assumed to be constant over time and, indeed, were regarded as subject to frequent change as a consequence of disequilibrating disturbances. In particular, they were not regarded as constant over time or as a stable function of some set of variable precisely because it was the nonstationarity of the system which is the source of interest rate risk. Thus, while at a given point in time liquidity premiums and term premiums can be regarded as formally equivalent, they are not substantively so. Liquidity premiums could be negative, a kind of solidity premium, if borrowers preferred to issue short-term debt while lenders' preferred habitats were long.[16] But term premiums must always be positive because of the empirical—not logical—circumstance that disequilibrating disturbances tend to produce positively correlated movement in successive one-period rates as the evidence presented later in this chapter strongly suggests. Having emphasized these differences, let us turn to the empirical work bearing on the liquidity preference hypothesis.

We may begin with an assessment of Meiselman's interpretation of his finding that the constant terms in the equations he fitted were not significantly different from zero. Meiselman reasoned that if there were liquidity premiums the constant terms should be significantly negative, reflecting their existence. To see this, consider the error term $E_t = R_{1,t} - F_{1,t-1,t}$. $F_{1,t-1,t}$ would be, following Eq. 4-5, equal to $R_{1,t-1,t} + L_{1,t-1,t}$ if liquidity premiums existed. Since, again following Eq. 4-5, $R_{1,t}$ contains no liquidity premium, the error term would be zero only when $R_{1,t}$ exceeded $r_{1,t-1,t}$ by $L_{1,t-1,t}$, which is to say if $R_{1,t} = r_{1,t-1,t}$ an error term equal to $L_{1,t-1,t}$ would appear. To keep the revision process from getting underway when, in fact, expectations were realized, a constant term equal to $-L_{1,t-1,t}$ would be required. This would just offset the appearance of $L_{1,t-1,t}$ as an error term and prevent the revision of forecasts of the $r_{1,t,t+m}$.

Both R. Kessel [32] and J. Wood [69] saw that this interpreta-

---

[16] For an example of this line of reasoning, see M. Bailey [2].

tion was inadequate. Consider that $\Delta r_{1,t,t+n}$ under the liquidity preference hypothesis would be equal to $(r_{1,t-1,t+n} + L_{1,t-1,t+n}) - (r_{1,t,t+n} + L_{1,t,t+n}) > 0$. $r_{1,t-1,t+n} = r_{1,t,t+n}$ because $L_{1,t-1,t+n} > L_{1,t,t+n}$ since $t + n$ is now one period closer and liquidity premiums decline as the period to which they are applicable becomes less distant. Thus it could happen that when, in fact, $R_{1,t} > r_{1,t-1,t}$ by $L_{1,t-1,t}$ so that the measured error term was zero, expectations were nevertheless revised, making $r_{1,t-1,t+n} > r_{1,t,t+n}$ by $(L_{1,t+n} - L_{1,t,t+n})$, the dependent and independent variable in the regression would be zero and, as a consequence, the constant term would be zero. Put differently, if liquidity premiums increase as the periods to which they are applicable recede into the future, Meiselman's constant terms might well be zero. It follows then, that Meiselman's results do not rule out the liquidity preference hypothesis.

It is important to note Meiselman's results do not "prove" the liquidity preference hypothesis either. It is entirely possible, as suggested above, these results merely reflect the fact that generally unanticipated disturbances tend to produce concomitant, parallel shifts in forecasts of many successive one-period rates. Moreover, it would appear that if we are to take the Kessel-Wood criticism seriously for tests utilizing time series data, especially spanning a period of fifty years or so, liquidity premiums must be regarded as fairly stable. In terms of the term premium hypothesis this would mean that the term premiums, the formal counterpart of the liquidity premiums, ought to be stable—which would appear to be evidence against the term premium hypothesis. From a slightly different point of view, proponents of the liquidity preference hypothesis should show that liquidity premiums are either constant or a stable function of a few variables or, at the very least, that they can be measured. With these caveats in mind let us turn to the evidence offered by the proponents of the liquidity preference hypothesis.

Kessel followed Meiselman's lead, adapting the error-learning mechanism to test the liquidity preference hypothesis. He was willing to interpret forward rates as estimators of subsequent spot rates; however, he was unwilling to accept Meiselman's view that because forecasts can prove wrong, subsequent spot rates need bear no relationship to prior forward rates. Kessel reasons that while Meiselman's position that forecast need not be accurate is correct, forecast errors should not be systematically biased. He argues:

> ... given free entry and competition in securities markets, should not one expect to find a relationship between expectations as inferred from the term structure of interest rates and subsequently observed actual rates? It is of course unreasonable to expect expectations or predictions of future short-term rates to be absolutely accurate. New informa-

tion coming to the market after a prediction is made will lead to prediction revisions and less than perfect forecasts. Yet new information
should not lead to biases in the estimates; a mean bias should not be
present. Hence, the average difference between predicted and actual
rates ought to be insignificantly different from zero. The absence or
presence of a mean bias in the relationship constitutes a test of whether
or not forward rates are expected rates. Similarly, for very short
intervals between the inference of predictions and the observation of
actual short-term rates, there should be some observable advantage for
the expectations hypothesis over some form of inertia hypothesis as a
predictor of future short rates. If not, why should the market waste its
time and energy, which are scarce resources, in trying to predict future
short-term rates? [32, p. 23]

As for the question why the market should devote scarce resources to forecasting, the argument presented in Chapter 3, that
there will be no relation between market prices and the underlying
real and policy variables unless portfolio managers do devote time
and energy to forecasting, appears to be an appropriate answer.
Turning to Kessel's empirical work, to test whether the average difference between predicted and actual rates was different from zero,
Kessel compared forward and actual yields of Treasury bills for the
period beginning January 1959 through March 1962. He picked this
period because at the beginning and end of the period the 91-day bill
rate was at the same level, 2.75 percent, though it had risen above
and fallen below this level during the period. By choosing this period
he believed he could control for trend and exclude the effects of
capital gains and losses. We shall call this belief into question
shortly.

Kessel's procedure was equivalent to applying Meiselman's error-
learning mechanism to the data to determine whether, for successive
trials within the period, the error term differed significantly from
zero. Thus, the forward 14-day rate was computed from observed 28-
day and 14-day rates. This forward rate was then compared to the
actual 14-day rate 14 days later and the difference observed. Comparisons were made also for 28-day, 42-day, 56-day, 63-day and 91-
day rates.[17] The average difference between forward and subsequent
spot rates was positive for all six series, which is to say in Kessel's
terms that forward rates are biased and high estimators of subsequent
spot rates.

---

[17]There were 82 successive two-week intervals in the period studied while
Kessel reports 124 observations of 14-day rates. Similarly, he reports 125 observations of 91-day rates whereas there were only 9 successive 13-week intervals.
The observations thus overlap. What this means for the interpretation of Kessel's
result is not made clear. The time series data discussed in the next section of this
chapter is free from this kind of interdependence.

This result, then, seems to confirm the liquidity preference hypothesis as given in Eq. 4-6; that is, the $L_{n,t,s}$ are positive. However, if liquidity premiums are to rise monotonically, as Kessel argued in his criticism of Meiselman's interpretation of the constant term in the latter's regressions, the average error should increase as the time spanned increases. However they do not do so in a clear-cut way. Taking the mean error as a measure of liquidity premiums, Kessel found the 14-day premium to be .199 percent, 28-day—.567 percent, 42-day—.599 percent, 56-day—.444 percent, 63-day—.455 percent, and 91-day—.669 percent. The failure of the means to rise monatomically suggests that we should not be too quick to interpret Kessel's findings as suggesting the liquidity preference hypothesis.

More specifically, a time series of error terms such as Kessel measured need not contain only errors generated by a stationary process as Kessel believes; in fact, some of the errors may be produced by departures from stationarity, which is to say, may result from changes in capital value. In terms of the preceding discussion, the liquidity premiums might not be stable. If so, further reasoning is necessary to specify the proper relationship between the mean errors just noted. Kessel does not recognize this difficulty.[18]   However, he does not believe liquidity premiums remain constant over time. Instead, he proposes the hypothesis that liquidity premiums are a stable function of the level of rates and so should vary over the cycle, increasing during booms and decreasing during recessions.

Kessel offers the following account of how liquidity premiums behave over the cycle:

> Economists customarily think of a rise in interest rates as implying an increase in the cost of holding money. By parity of reasoning, an increase in interest rates should also imply an increase in the cost of holding substitutes. . . .   Such a rise implies an increase in liquidity premiums, i.e., an increase in the spread between forward and [subsequent spot rates]. [32, p. 25]

To test this, Kessel, using his Treasury bill data, regressed the difference between forward and subsequent spot rates on the level of current spot rates and found the difference to increase as the level of the

---

[18] As noted above, he selected this period "to control for trends in rates, and to measure forward and actual rates uninfluenced by capital gains considerations" [32, p. 23].   Kessel assumes that windfall gains and losses occurring during the period will offset each other.   He does not demonstrate that they will nor is he aware of the kind of evidence presented below on time series of realized holding period yields which suggest that they are not likely to offset each other unless the period observed is selected to make the cumulated windfalls cancel. But even if this could be done readily, it would not mean that liquidity premiums would then be measured because this offsetting would not, indeed could not, insure stationarity. We will return to these points below.

current rate increased.[19] However, these results are well-behaved only for the bill data; data from series on long-term yields to maturity do not support the notion that liquidity premiums are a stable function of the level of rates.[20]

What I wish to take issue with here is not these findings but rather certain aspects of Kessel's interpretation of them. Much of what he found is paralleled by other findings to be presented shortly. Kessel interprets these results as consistent with the liquidity premium hypothesis with its hedger-speculator dichotomy, homogeneous expectations and treatment of the system as, generally, a stationary one.[21] I wish to shift the perspective from one in which positive liquidity premiums arise from a constitutional weakness to one in which term premiums arise because of the nonstationarity and and uncertainty of the system. From the latter perspective we can see the role of speculative activity as one of making the market possible rather than causing the market to be actuated as if by an error-learning mechanism. In particular, I wish to show why liquidity premiums cannot be estimated in the way Kessel supposes.

Regarding Kessel's findings that liquidity premiums are positive functions of the level of rates, it may be noted first that this is inconsistent with his critique of Meiselman's interpretation of his zero constant term. Recall that Kessel (and Wood) argued that a zero constant term is not inconsistent with the existence of liquidity premiums. However, this can be true only if the liquidity premiums are stable, or at least remain proportional, over time, and are independent of the level of rates. If these conditions were not met Meiselman's interpretation could not be subjected to this line of criticism because there would be no reason for the impact of liquidity premiums on the revision term to offset its impact on the error term—the dependent and independent variables respectively—in Meiselman's regressions.[22]

[19] Kessel [32, p. 26].

[20] Kessel [32, pp. 32–33] reports that for rates, longer-term rates, for example, one and two-year rates, the relation between the level of liquidity premiums (the bias in forward rates derived by comparison with subsequent spot rates) and the level of current rates becomes much less clear. Thus, "in the case of one and two-year governments, [the regression coefficient] is positive but only nine-tenths its standard error."

[21] Kessel shows some awareness of the nonstationarity of the system when he reports that during upswings spot rates are sometimes "in excess of forward rates" [32, p. 23]. Below it is argued that when rates are rising, they typically rise more than had been expected producing windfall losses. For spot rates to be in excess of forward rates in the context of Kessel's comparison, windfall losses must have occurred so that the stationarity assumed by him is violated.

[22] Telser [62, p. 599] comments on some of these difficulties. He notes that Kessel's regression show strong autocorrelation in the residuals which leads him "to suspect the omission of some important factors that are themselves auto-correlated." See also Van Horne [66] and Roll [56].

More fundamental in my view is the fact that mean error of Kessel's six comparisons does not reveal a consistent pattern of increase as term to maturity increases. As has been suggested, if portfolio managers are to revise according to Meiselman's error-learning mechanism they must be able to remove the effects of liquidity premiums so that they can tell when their (homogeneous) expectations are in error. How can they do that if liquidity premiums cannot be estimated with any confidence by independent investigators?[23] My contention is that they cannot be measured because of the nonstationarity of the system. The following discussions present some reasoning and data to support this contention.

C. HOLDING-PERIOD YIELDS: SOME EVIDENCE ON NONSTATIONARITY

A holding period, as used in Chapter 1, was defined as a finite time span over which a yield may be contemplated generally distinct and separate from the period spanned by a term to maturity. It will be convenient here to present a version of the time path of a perpetuity to show how holding-period yields relate to forward rates and expected one-period rates under both the expectations and liquidity preference hypotheses before turning to the holding-period findings. Once the mechanics are made clear we can turn to substantive issues. Figure 4-1 shows two time paths of a discounted perpetuity over the two periods prior to reaching equilibrium. The upper time path corresponds to the certainty case and here represents the expectations hypothesis since, as we have seen, it deals with uncertainty essentially by making it equivalent to certainty. The lower time path represents the liquidity preference hypothesis. V'_e is placed below V_e to permit the graphical exposition: the slopes are critical here, not the levels. If $V'_e = V_e$ then $V_0 > V'_0$, which is to say that liquidity preference reduces the price of the two-period note below what it would be under certainty or under the expectations hypothesis.

The ratio of $V_e/V_0 = (1 + R_{2,0})^2$, the holding-period yield on a discounted perpetuity over the two periods. $V_1/V_0 = 1 + R_{1,0}$, the holding-period yield over one period on a discounted perpetuity. Under the expectations hypothesis, $R_{1,0}$ and $R_{2,0}$ are the yield to maturity on one and two-period discounted notes respectively. $V_e/V_1 = 1 +$

[23] It could be argued that the market behaves "as if" portfolio managers knew what liquidity premiums were so that they could know when their identical expectations turned out to be in error. Not only does this beg the question of how information on the underlying variables influences expectations, but it presumes that the market conforms to the error-learning mechanism and we have seen that this conformation is far from perfect.

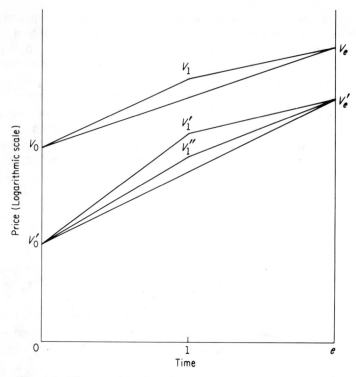

Fig. 4-1. Time paths of a discounted perpetuity under the expectations and the liquidity preference hypotheses. The upper path corresponds to the former, the lower path to the latter hypothesis.

$r_{1,0,2}$, the one-period rate to rule in period 2. Under the expectations hypothesis $F_{1,0,2} = r_{1,0,2}$. Turning to the lower time path, the two-period yield to maturity is $V_e'/V_0' = 1 + R_{2,0}'$. The one-period yield to maturity under the liquidity preference hypothesis, following Eq. 4-5 will be $R_{1,0}$ as represented by V_1''/V_0'. This result obtains because, by convention, we define the one-period rate as free of a liquidity premium.

Using $R_{1,0}$ and $R_{2,0}'$ we can show $F_{2,0,1}'$ as in Eq. 4-6 is equal to $r_{1,0,1} + L_{1,0,1}$. Thus, the difference in the slope of V_1'/V_e and V_1''/V_e' measures the liquidity premium. Corresponding to this divergence is the one between V_1'/V_0' and V_1''/V_0' which represent respectively the holding-period yields on a two-period note over the first period and the holding-period yield on a one-period note over the first period. Thus, under the liquidity preference hypothesis the expected yield on a two-period note over the first period must exceed the expected yield on a one-period note over the same period.

We may define a holding-period yield on an n-period note over period t as seen at time t as follows:

(4-7)
$$1 + H_{n,t} = \frac{(1 + R_{n,t})^n}{(1 + r_{1,t+1,\,t+1}) \cdots (1 + r_{1,\,t+1,\,t+n-1})}$$

$$= \frac{(1 + R_{1,t}) \cdots (1 + r_{1,\,t,\,t+n-1} + L_{1,t,\,t+n-1})}{(1 + r_{1,\,t+1,\,t+1}) \cdots (1 + r_{1,\,t+1,\,t+n-1})}$$

The presence of the liquidity premiums in the numerator which increase as the time to the period to which they apply increases means that under the liquidity preference hypotheses

(4-8) $$R_{1,t} = H_{1,t} < H_{2,t} < \cdots < H_{n,t}$$

Under the expectations hypothesis all $L_{1,t,s}$ are zero so that

(4-9) $$R_{1,t} = H_{1,t} = H_{2,t} = \cdots = H_{n,t} \text{[24]}$$

Now if Kessel's argument is correct, that observed security prices are generated by a stationary process such that "new information should not lead to biases in the estimates [implicit in forward rates of subsequent spot rates]," time series of realized holding period on securities with different terms to maturity ought to be equal if the expectations hypothesis is correct and unequal as given by Eq. 4-8 if the liquidity preference hypothesis is correct. In the terms just developed, to say that $F_{1,0,2}$ can be compared to $R_{1,1}$ to distinguish between the two hypotheses is formally identical to saying that an observed holding-period yield on a two-period note over the first period can be compared to $R_{1,0}$.[25]

However, we need not be bound by any notion of how forecasts are made or revised. In a stationary system we may posit simply that forecasts tend to be realized but not perfectly. Thus, let us define a realized holding-period yield on an n-period security as follows:

(4-10) $$Y_{n,t} = H_{n,t} + u_{n,t}$$

Where the $H_{n,t}$ is the yield over period t expected by the market on a security maturing at the end of n-periods and $u_{n,t}$ is a normally distributed random disturbance with mean zero. By observing the means of a number of time series of realized yields having different

[24] See J. Conard [12] for a fuller discussion of holding-period yields.

[25] It is important to recognize that expected holding-period yields cannot be observed directly. However, following Kessel's assumption of a stationary generating process, realized holding-period yields will differ from their anticipated counterparts only because of "noise" in the system. As sample size increases, the effects of this noise will tend to wash out.

terms to maturity, it should be possible, if Kessel is right, to determine whether the expectations or liquidity preference hypothesis best explains the data.

Before turning to the results from a time series analysis of this kind, it is important to take explicit account of the effects of disturbances; that is, of nonstationarity or of what Meiselman would call changes in "the interest rate." Realized yields over periods during which such disturbances produce windfall price changes may be expressed as

(4-11) $Y_{n,t} = \beta_{n,t}$

where $\beta_{n,t}$ is windfall change in price occurring during period t of a security maturing at the end of n periods. $\beta_{n,t}$ may be positive or negative. Unlike the $u_{n,t}$ in Eq. 4-10, there is no reason to assume the $\beta_{n,t}$ to be normally distributed with a mean value of zero.

The disturbance term $u_{n,t}$ represents the noise generated by a process the controlling parameters of which are stable. Thus, the noise can be regarded as the consequence of random disturbances no one of which is large and which, following the central limit theorem, will be normally disturbed. The shock term $\beta_{n,t}$ represents shifts in the parameters, in the present case shifts in the underlying variables listed at end of Chapter 2, which control the growth in price of a discounted security as maturity approaches. Such terms are not likely to be normally distributed because some of these disturbances are likely to be large. In particular observations of this kind are likely to be distributed according to the "Statistical Law of Pareto."[26] Paretian variables have infinite population variances. The variances of samples of Paretian variables do not tend to a limit but are unstable. One form this instability could take in time series data is secular drift.

What does this imply for the kind of holding-period test implicit in Kessel's mean forecasting error approach? It may mean, as Mandelbrot has suggested that we may be faced with "a burden of proof that is closer to that of history and autobiography than to that of physics" [40, p. 433]. In the terms of Kessel's work it may mean that there is no way "to measure forward and actual rates uninfluenced by capital gain considerations." Kessel's approach can only be applied data which arises from the process implied in Eq. 4-10.

What can be done if the times series of $Y_{n,t}$ available to make the holding-period tests contain an admixture of realized yields of the

---

[26] See B. Mandelbrot [40] for a discussion of the Pareto-Levy family of distributions. The normal distribution is a special case of this family. It is the only member which has a finite variance.

kind described by Eq. 4-11; that is, reflecting the impact of shifts in parameters? It is conceivable that the data reflecting $\beta_{n,t}$ are sufficiently infrequent and readily identifiable to permit their elimination, leaving relatively large samples of $Y_{n,t}$ for which the $H_{n,t}$ are undisturbed. Recall that a shock may change the level as well as the structure of rates so that the samples of realized yields for differing maturity must be drawn from the same disturbance-free span of time. However, it may not be possible to eliminate such "contaminated" data from a time series. If not, direct tests of Kessel's kind become problematic.

Moreover, if data reflecting the $\beta_{n,t}$ occur frequently and cannot be easily distinguished from data reflecting the $H_{n,t}$, this situation becomes more than problematic. What is called into question is the stationary framework within which both the expectations and liquidity preference hypotheses are cast. Put differently, if the market is best characterized as subject to such frequent disturbance that liquidity premiums cannot be measured, it may be more useful to view it in terms of the term premium hypothesis, based, as it is, on a model of portfolio management aimed at coping with a nonstationary environment. Let us now turn to the realized holding-period yield data.

The results reported below were obtained from time series of realized yields constructed from the Friday closing quotations on Treasury bills and bonds for the period beginning January, 1951, and ending December, 1962, 625 weeks in all.[27] The bill series range in maturity from one to thirteen weeks and the bond series from 2.5 years to greater than 15 years. Realized holding-period yields were derived from these prices by computing the logarithms of successive price relatives on individual securities as follows:

$$(4\text{-}12) \qquad Y_{n,t} = \log \left[\frac{(V_{n,t+1} + C_{n,t+1})}{(V_{n,t} + C_{n,t})} \right]$$

where the $Y_{n,t}$ is the realized yield as in Eqs. 4-10 and 4-11, and $V_{n,t+1}$ the price on a given Friday, $V_{n,t}$ the price on the preceding Friday, the $C_{n,t+1}$ the prorated value of the coupon (on bonds) on a given Friday, and $C_{n,t}$ the prorated value of the coupon on the preceding Friday.[28] From these observations eighteen time series were

[27] The data and procedures are more fully described in Michaelsen [45]. The relationship of holding-period yields to Kessel's tests was noted after this study was virtually completed.

[28] Logarithms were used because we are interested in rates of change, rather than absolute changes, in prices. If the $Y_{n,t}$ were distributed normally, in the absence of logarithms the ratio would be log-normally distributed. It is easier to work with normal than log-normal distributions. However, as we shall see, the

constructed, one for each maturity from one through 13 weeks from the Treasury bill data and one each for maturities ranging from 2.5, 5, 7.5 and 10 years and two for maturities longer than 15 years from the Treasury bond data. Finally, bill and bond indexes were constructed as unweighted averages of the 13 bill and six bond series respectively.

If the data is generated by a stationary process, the means of all series should be equal (supporting the expectations hypothesis) or rise as term to maturity of the series increases (suggesting the liquidity preference hypothesis). The results presented in Table 4-2 show the difference between the mean of the one-week and the 13-week series to be positive for the entire period and for each of the subperiods as demarcated by the National Bureau of Economic Research reference cycle turning points into cyclical upturns and downturns. This same difference is found between each adjacent pair of the 13 bill series for the entire period and for each subperiod with some minor exceptions.[29] However, this is not true for the bond series as shown by the means of the bond index, which, while 2.00 percent for the period as a whole, alternate widely over the cycle.

If the liquidity preference hypothesis as advanced by Kessel is correct, and ignoring for the moment the means of the bond index, the spread between the one and 13-week series of .83 annual percentage points is an estimate of the liquidity premium in the forward 13-week rate which compares to Kessel's estimate of .669 annual percentage points.[30] While these estimates are close, we should examine the cyclical behavior of the spreads before accepting these findings as supporting Kessel's views. Kessel found that his forecasting errors were positively related to the current rate and interpreted

---

$Y_{n,t}$ do not appear to be normally distributed. The $C_{n,t}$ has to be added because most bonds, including government issues, are not traded flat as in common stock. For the latter, dividends belong to the buyer, except after the date the stock goes ex-dividend. For bonds, there is a fiction that the buyer must pay the seller for the coupon in addition to the face value. Thus, bond quotations do not include the price of the coupon, whereas stock quotations include the price of the dividend. The $V_{n,t}$ are the mean of the corresponding bid and ask quotations.

[29] See Michaelsen [45, p. 454]. The mean for the 11- and 12-week series does not display this rising pattern consistently.

[30] The .83 figure represents the holding-period yield differential and the .669 figure the liquidity premium which, as Fig. 4-1 shows, are equivalent. However, the periods spanned by the two figures are not the same. Holding-period differentials could reflect chiefly transaction costs that rise with term to maturity. To test this, estimates of differentials were made on the assumption that the security was purchased at the ask quotation at the beginning of the week and sold at the bid quotation at the end of the week instead of at the mean of these two quotations. The differential narrows but does not vanish, suggesting that transaction costs need not be given great weight.

TABLE 4-2

Means of Time Series of Realized Yields on Selected Treasury Bills and Bonds for the 625-Week Period Beginning January 5, 1951 and Ending December 28, 1962 and for Selected Subperiods[a]

(Figures in annual percentages)

Series by Term to Maturity (1)	Entire Period 1/5/51 12/28/62 T-P (2)	Subperiods						
		1/5/51 7/3/53 T-P (3)	7/3/53 8/6/54 P-T (4)	8/6/54 7/5/57 T-P (5)	7/5/57 4/3/58 P-T (6)	4/3/58 5/13/60 T-P (7)	5/13/60 2/3/61 P-T (8)	2/3/61 12/28/62 T-P (9)
1 Week	1.69	1.24	0.79	1.70	2.37	2.12	1.69	2.03
13 Week	2.52	1.88	1.71	2.29	3.94	3.10	3.37	2.67
13 Week minus 1 Week	0.83	0.64	0.92	0.59	1.57	0.98	1.68	0.64
Bond Index	2.00	0.06	7.93	-1.65	13.77	-1.64	7.64	4.02

[a]Subperiods are either upturns (T-P) or downturns (P-T) as given by NBER reference cycle turning points. January 5, 1951 and December 28, 1962 are not turning points.

this as showing that liquidity premiums are positively related to the level of rates. Yet the spread row, (the 13-week minus 1-week row,) in Table 4-2 suggests a different relationship. Thus, when the mean of the 13-week series declines from column (3) to column (4), the spread increases, whereas as the mean increases from column (4) to column (5) the spread declines. This pattern is reversed for the later subperiods. Thus, the spread increases as the level of the 13-week mean increases as we move from columns (5) to (6) to (7) to (8). At the very least, this does not suggest a stationary process.

However, another pattern can be seen if the level of rates, as measured by the mean of the 13-week series, is ignored; which is to say, if we abandon Kessel's explanation of the variation in liquidity premiums as caused by the level of rates. Thus, the spread between the one and 13-week series is greater during downturns in business activity than it is during the preceding and the subsequent upturns. A similar pattern is true of means of the bond index. One interpretation of this cyclical pattern is that during upturns, rates rise, but the extent of the rise is not fully anticipated so windfall price declines predominate. During downturns rates fall, again more than was generally anticipated producing windfall price increases. In terms of Eq. 4-11 the $\beta_{n,t}$ are more frequently large and negative during upturns, and large and positive during downturns.[31]

If this interpretation is correct, and it is consistent with the general argument which has been made about the fundamental role of nonstationarity in the determination of the structure and level of interest rates since it sees recurrent shocks to the system as a central phenomenon, the shorter-term bill series are "contaminated" with $\beta_{n,t}$. For very short-term securities, the windfalls do not swamp the force of expectations—the spread between the one and 13-week bill series always remains positive during upturns. The $\beta_{n,t}$ introduce an unknown bias so that the spread between one and 13-week bill series cannot be taken as estimates of the corresponding liquidity premiums. Moreover, since the level of rates is not constant during each subperiod, the $H_{n,t}$ of Eq. 4-10 are not constant either so that even if the effects of the $\beta_{n,t}$ could be removed, the remaining estimate would be an average of changing holding-period yields and so would still present measurement problems, though these would not be insurmountable. Since no way is presently available to identify only those observations resulting from shifts in parameters, there is no way

[31] Given this cyclical behavior of windfall price changes it is clear that Kessel's forecasting error is subject to an unknown bias. Consequently, his interpretation of his regression of forecastīng errors on the level of current rates as showing how liquidity premiums vary over the cycle cannot be taken at face value.

to estimate liquidity premiums. If disinterested investigators cannot estimate them it is hard to believe that portfolio managers who speculate can do it in such a way that each of them has the same estimates of liquidity premium and the same expectations about future one-period rates.

Whatever tendency toward steady-state equilibrium that may be apparent in the bill series, no such tendency toward orderly structure can be found in the bond series. The mean of the bonds index can hardly be said to approximate a holding-period yield since these are negative during two upturns and nearly zero during one.[32] The means of the individual bond series behave similarly, the longer-term means usually showing wider variation over the cycle. To argue this is not to argue that expectation and aversion to risk do not influence the structure of yields at a given point in time. As we have seen, liquidity premiums, holding-period yield differential and term premiums are logically equivalent when considered in a comparative static framework. The findings on the bill series mean thus support the term premium hypothesis. What these results do not do is suggest that longer-term security prices reflect homogeneous expectations.

Before leaving the means of these series some note should be taken of their implications for the results of portfolio management policies. Consider, say, a life insurance company which, over the period, maintained a stable volume of insurance business, meeting maturing liabilities with premium inflows. Suppose its portfolio manager could forecast no better than chance and so maintained a very short-term asset portfolio, purchasing, say, 26-week bills to replace maturing ones so that the realized holding-period yield on the portfolio was 2.52 percent per annum. Had he adopted the same policy, but maintained an average maturity of roughly 7.5 years, he would have shown a realized holding-period yield on the portfolio of approximately 2 percent per annum![33] Being long—more nearly in the preferred habitat—would have produced less return for the firm's shareholders than being further away from its preferred habitat.

For different periods the result achieved by such an extrapolating portfolio manager could well be different.[34] This is one of the important implications of the nonnormality of the $\beta_{n,t}$: there will be no stable mean of zero around which the effects of shocks will tend to

[32] The last subperiod is not a complete upturn so that the meaning to be attached to the mean of the bond index is unclear.

[33] This is the mean of the bond index.

[34] The results for the most recent 12-year period might well show the short-term portfolio to have produced an even greater excess over the realized yield to an extrapolating long-term portfolio because of accelerating secular rise in the level of rates in recent years.

fall.   Moreover, whatever the apparent pattern, both secular and cyclical, before the fact the future is uncertain, otherwise windfalls could not occur.   It is well to recall Mandelbrot's suggestion that analytical problems here parallel more closely that of history or evolution rather than of physics or functional time.

Other aspects of the behavior of these time series bear on the issue we are considering.   These are (1) the characteristics of their dispersion, including their standard deviations; (2) the intercorrelation between them; and (3) their serial correlations.   Let us begin with the findings on dispersion.   If the market were in a steady-state equilibrium, Eq. 4-10 would characterize the process giving rise to these time series.   Their dispersion would be the dispersion of the $u_{n,t}$.   It is possible that σ_{n_t} would rise as n rose; however, the distribution should be normal and its standard duration should never be so large as to swamp the $H_{n,t}$.   If, say, the standard deviation were five to ten times the series mean, the process would appear as dominated by disturbances and the differences between series means and between series means and zero would be extremely difficult to establish.

However, if the market were usually responding to shifts in underlying variables, Eq. 4-11 would characterize the process giving rise to these time series.   Their dispersion would be chiefly the dispersion of the $\beta_{n,t}$.   Because successive one-period rates tend to shift in the same direction in response to shifts in underlying variables, the $\beta_{n,t}$ should increase as n increases.   Consequently, $\sigma_{\beta_{n,t}}$ should increase as term to maturity increases.   How does the dispersion of $\beta_{n,t}$ then differ from that of the $u_{n,t}$?   First, the standard deviations will become large relative to the means of the series, virtually swamping the means.   Second, the distribution will not be normal, but will have too many extreme observations in the tails—the tails will be "too fat."   Another consequence of nonnormality is that the standard deviations of samples will vary over time.

The standard deviations of the bill and bond series rise monotonically with term to maturity.   The difference in magnitude of this statistic between the long- and short-term series is considerable; the standard deviation of the bill index is 1.21 percent per annum while that for the bond index 23.24 percent per annum.   The standard deviation of the bill index is small relative to its mean of 2.23 percent.   The bill series behave as if generated by steady-state process (except for the presence of windfall effects discussed above under the behavior of the means).   By contrast, most of the observations in the bond index series are considerably larger in absolute value than the bond index mean of 2.00 percent. The longer-term series behave as if generated by a nonstationary process.

Furthermore, the standard deviations display no cyclical pattern and appear to drift over time, increasing from subperiod to subperiod up through the 1958–1960 upturn and declining thereafter. By standard tests for the equality of variances this secular drift appears to be significant; the variances differed significantly among sub-periods. Finally, the distributions of the bond series appeared to have "fat" tails.[35] Thus, the evidence goes against the steady-state assumption.

Turning now to the intercorrelations, the steady-state and non-stationary process models have similar implications, but differ markedly from the segmented market hypothesis which asserts markets for different maturities to be virtually unconnected.[36] Since the behavior of the means and standard deviations suggest the dominance of nonstationarity, we will concentrate on the implications of Eq. 4-11 as compared to those of the segmented market hypothesis for the intercorrelations between the series. Following the argument that shifts in successive one-period rates will be positively, though not perfectly, correlated, and that expectations significantly influence portfolio behavior, we should find that inter-correlation between series increases as the time spanned in common increases since the closer together these terms to maturity are, the greater the number of common elements shared between them.[37] The segmented market hypothesis suggests, if anything, that the relationship between price movement on securities with different maturities should be unrelated; that is, time series of the present kind should be independent.

The correlations coefficients between the seven series, including

---

[35] Because the bills series display strong serial dependence their distributions cannot be easily determined. This dependence is discussed below.

[36] If Eq. 4-10 described the process, variation in the level of rates of the cycle would cause the series to be positively intercorrelated. If Eq. 4-11 described the process, the effects of disturbance common to many series would cause them to be positively intercorrelated.

[37] One way to see this is to express changes in the price of bond as the relationship between its yield to maturity prior to a disturbance $R_{n,t}$ to its yield to just afterward, $\dot{R}_{n,t}$. Thus, including expected rates only,

$$\frac{(1 + R_{n,t})}{(1 + \dot{R}_{n,t})} = \frac{(1 + R_{1,t})(1 + r_{1,2,t}) \cdots (1 + r_{1,n-1,t})}{(1 + \dot{R}_{1,t})(1 + \dot{r}_{1,2,t}) \cdots (1 + \dot{r}_{1,n-1,t})}$$

If many, but not all of the $\dot{r}_{1,n,t} \gtrless r_{1,n,t}$ then, as between securities with differing maturities, of the periods they have in common, the more terms, $1 + r_{1,n,t} / 1 + \dot{r}_{1,n,t}$, they will have in common, and hence the greater their intercorrelation, A ratio of unity means no price change and hence no basis for correlation.

the 13-week bill series and the six bond series appear in Table 4-3. The tendency for the coefficients to increase as terms to maturity of the series compared become more nearly equal is quite apparent. The coefficients rise as we move down the columns, and fall as we move across the rows. This tendency is pronounced in the change in the coefficients between the 2.5- and 5-year series—.676—and the 5- and 7.5-year—.802. The markets for securities of different maturities appear to be related in the way suggested by the term premium hypothesis.

TABLE 4-3

Correlation Coefficients between Time Series of Realized Yields on Selected Treasury Bills and Bonds for the Period Beginning January 5, 1951 and Ending December 28, 1962

Series by Term to Maturity	13 Week	2.5 Year	5 Year	10 Year	Year	Long 1	Long 2
13 Week	1.000	.333	.291	.277	.251	.260	.271
2.5 Year		1.000	.676	.618	.593	.592	.554
5 Year			1.000	.802	.724	.718	.699
7.5 Year				1.000	.809	.720	.735
10 Year					1.000	.726	.721
Long 1						1.000	.861
Long 2							1.000

Moreover, this pattern of intercorrelation can explain the decline in Meiselman's regression and correlation coefficients reported in Table 4-3. According to the term premium hypothesis forecasts of successive one-period rates will usually, but not always move in the same direction in response to shifts in the underlying variables. This hypothesis, unlike Meiselman's, does not explain the correlation as part of error-revision mechanisms unrelated to the empirical relationship among these variables. Consequently, the question of the substantive interrelationship involved in forecasting is left open. But, whatever these may be, if the correlations between changes in successive rates is positive but not perfect, the correlation between price changes on securities of different maturities will be positive, but not perfect. The decline in Meiselman's coefficient as term to maturity is due in a literal sense to the fact that movements in one-year bond prices are more highly correlated with movements in two-year bond prices than with those in eight-year bond prices. This is precisely what the decline in the coefficients across the 13-week period in Table 4-3 reflect. Thus, it would appear that not only do we lack a theory of how forecasts are initially made, but we also lack a theory of how forecasts are revised.

Finally, we may consider the serial dependence in the time series. Steady-state time series would display no serial dependence only if the level of rates were constant. If this were so, and successive $u_{n,t}$ were independent, serial correlation coefficients would be zero since they would be measuring the time dependence of noise.[38] If the level of rates followed a cyclical pattern and this pattern were fully anticipated, the time series would display strong positive serial correlation. A nonstationary series, however, would display no serial dependence, which is to say changes in prices could not be predicted by extrapolating past changes in prices. This is not to say that price changes, the $\beta_{n,t}$, cannot be predicted: speculators seeking gains from superior forecasting techniques using information they have acquired with some difficulty, could and, indeed, must do this if security prices are to reflect opportunity costs as we have seen.[39] Rather, it is to argue that simple, or even complex, mechanical extrapolation will be of no avail in a market where nonstationarity is a central feature.[40]

The bill series display strong serial dependence.[41] This dependence shows the considerable extent to which the short end of the market reflects a coalescence of expectation about the course of short-term rates over the near term future. This finding parallels those reported above on the behavior of bill series means, standard deviations and intercorrelations, all of which were interpreted as due to many (not all) realized yields for these series arising from an approximately steady-state process. The bond series display almost no serial dependence. Long-term bond price movements do appear to follow the random walk pattern in which subsequent steps or movements cannot be predicted from the pattern of past movements. This finding, together with the others just discussed, strongly suggest that longer-term security price changes are generated by a nonstationary, rather than a steady-state process.

It will be helpful at this point to summarize the conclusions

[38] Serial correlation coefficients for these series were derived by lagging the series one observation (for first order coefficients) and treating the original and lagged series as two series just as the series were treated in computing the intercorrelations in Table 4-3.

[39] Past price data is public and virtually free, though it is costly to manipulate on computers. Still, compared to getting information on the underlying variables, processing price data must be regarded as trival. It would be unlikely to contain information of particular value.

[40] If price changes are random walk, past price behavior contains no useful information. For a review of literature on the random walks hypothesis in security markets, see E. Fama [19]. See also R. Roll [56] for an application of the random walk model to the Treasury Bill Market.

[41] See Michaelsen [45, p. 459].

reached about the evidence reviewed so far:

1. Expectations about the course of the level of rates influence prices. Very little can be said about how forecasts are made or about how they are revised. In particular, a market-wide error-learning revision mechanism does not appear to offer a fruitful approach to the question of how portfolios collect and process information bearing on the demand for funds in future periods.

2. Prices of securities are lower than they would be if portfolio managers were indifferent to interest rate risk. The Kessel liquidity premiums are formally equivalent to the term premiums of the term premium hypothesis. Even though a significant tendency for short-term realized holding-period yields to display the steady-state differential predicted by the liquidity preference hypothesis was apparent, the situation was too unstable to permit the precise measurement of holding-period yield differentials. It remains to be demonstrated that stable liquidity premiums exist in forward rates applicable to the near term future.

3. Longer-term realized holding-period yields do not display even this tendency toward a steady-state equilibrium. The behavior of these longer-term yields is consistent with the implication of the term premium hypothesis that the process generating long-term security price movements is a nonstationary one.

4. Interest rate risk rises, not because of departures from preferred habitats but because of this fundamental nonstationarity. The interpretation given to mean realized holding-period yield on the bond index shows that an insurance company that was "too short" but which could not forecast shifts in interest rates would have done better over the period studied than one which was in its preferred habitat. At the same time, it should be noted that over some different period the results could be reversed. This latter possibility is one consequence of nonstationarity.

chapter 5

Some Evidence on Interest Rate Forecasts and Forecasting Techniques

The conclusions just stated at the end of the previous chapter imply that if expectations could be directly observed for a cross section of portfolio managers, one would expect to find major divergences for rates applicable to more distant periods. We shall begin, in this chapter, with a review of some direct evidence of this kind which supports this implication. Next we shall consider some of the recent work which develops explicit models of interest rate forecasting. As we shall see, these models are aggregative, applying to "the market," and consequently, rather than explaining how such divergent views arise, render such divergences "harmless." These models offer little insight into how speculators speculate; rather they serve to show how extrapolators, in the sense described in Chapter 3, extrapolate. Finally, we will examine briefly some of the nonextrapolative techniques for forecasting interest rates. None of these results or techniques will lead us to abandon the notion of interest rate risk as arising from the nonstationarity of the system and the speculator-extrapolator hypotheses of portfolio management that flows from it.

A. SOME EVIDENCE ON THE HETEROGENEITY OF EXPECTATION

In a recent study [31] Kane and Malkiel provide some striking direct evidence on the extent to which expectations of future interest rates diverge.[1] They conducted a mail survey of a sample of firms—

[1] See B. Malkiel [38], especially Chapter 6, for similar direct evidence of institutional behavior.

the sample included 119 commercial banks, 16 life insurance companies and 65 nonfinancial corporations—likely to be active in the government securities market. Their aim was to get direct evidence on expectations as a means of testing term structure hypotheses. Consequently, they were not concerned with forecasting techniques but rather with the question of how forecasts, once made, influence portfolio decisions. Nevertheless, they did presume a kind of extrapolative forecasting model in their normal range hypothesis.

According to this hypothesis, portfolio managers "expect the historical range of past interest rates to prevail into the future and that, *lacking specific evidence to the contrary* (my italics), [they] tend to regard movement toward every rate in this range as equally likely" [31]. However, because Kane and Malkiel explicitly introduced, even insisted upon, the possibility of divergent expectations, speculative forecasting in the sense described in Chapter 3 is not precluded by their approach. The key here is "specific evidence"; what is crucial is what happens when such evidence is not lacking. Thus, in reviewing the Kane and Malkiel findings we can determine the extent to which they support indirectly the significance of the kind of speculative activity that is central to the term premium hypothesis.

A useful way to review their findings is to consider the five main conclusions they reached in the order they presented them.

1. While many investors seem to formulate specific interest-rate expectations, others do not. Significantly, differences in the willingness to predict follow institutional lines. In particular, banks are more likely to venture predictions than other institutions.

I have argued above that portfolio managers are likely to specialize in some class or classes of assets. Government securities as secondary reserves constitute a very considerable proportion of bank assets; consequently, banks would have an incentive to be concerned with movements in governmental securities prices. In addition, movements in the level of rates and monetary policy actions affect their liabilities as well as their assets. It should not be surprising, then, that large banks form explicit interest rate expectations.[2] Nonfinancial firms, for example, are much more likely to devote their forecasting effects toward estimating demand in their product markets and translating it into prospective returns to investment outlays. Put somewhat differently, banks do not specialize in forecasting particular final product markets in part because they are spread across such a wide variety of markets in their loan portfolios, but rather in

[2] Ninety-three percent of the banks which responded to the survey reported interest rate forecasts.

forecasting those factors which cut across these markets; that is in those factors which influence the level of all rates.

The life companies were next and the nonfinancial corporations last in the frequency of explicit forecasts of the rates specified in the survey-forward 90-day bill rates over a two-year period and 10-year bond rates one and two years into the future.[3] Following the reasoning in the previous paragraph, we would expect life companies to fall between banks and nonfinancial firms in their concern with the general level of rates.

> 2. The hypothesis that investors hold a uniform set of expectations of future interest rates is contradicted by the data.

A considerable range was observed for the estimates of each of the rates specified in the survey. As was already noted, no attempt was made to inquire into the forecasting techniques used. However, the observed divergence would be surprising if all the respondents used the same method of extrapolation from publicly available data. At the same time, past experience seemed to be important. Thus, the actual 10-year rates for both the April 1, 1966 and April 1, 1967 dates were well above the mean of estimates made of them on April 1, 1965.[4] Long-term government bond rates had not been as high as 4.5 percent since the early 1920's. It would be most instructive to observe how these forecasting errors were used by the respondents once they became apparent. In lieu of such evidence, we can say very little about the kinds of data that went into the making of these forecasts.[5]

> 3. Both willingness to predict and the extent of disagreement (the two dimensions of nonuniformity in expectations) vary with the futurity of the rate predicted.

The interpretation of the data on the means of the time series reported in Chapter 4 is consistent with this statement. I argued there that a consensus was more likely over the near-term future than over the longer-term. The fact that the means of the bill series displayed the same ordering—mean realized yields increasing as term to maturity of the bill series increased—during upturns and downturns was in-

---

[3] Sixty-seven percent of the life companies and 37 percent of the nonfinancial corporations which responded reported explicit forecasts. It should be noted that, following the reasoning presented in the first three chapters, the information needed to forecast the ten-year bond rate one and two years hence is the same as that required to forecast successive 90-day bill rates for eleven and twelve years into the future.

[4] The realized rate was roughly two standard deviations above the mean estimate in both instances.

[5] Data in their Table 4 reveals the wide diversity of forecasting errors reported by survey respondents.

terpreted to mean both that agreement was much greater and the amount of error much smaller for forecasts of short-term rates to rule in the near future. At the same time, forecasts of short-term rates to rule in the longer-term as evidenced by the behavior of the means of the bond series, are subject to greater error.

> 4. Our survey suggests that investors are influenced by their expecta-tions in deciding which maturity areas are attractive for purchase.

The survey does not reveal whether the respondents actually took positions which they said seemed especially attractive; conse-quently, we can only assume that they later took the speculative positions that they noted at the time of the survey. The most nota-ble example was that the respondents who found long-term securities relatively attractive showed a significantly lower mean expectation of long-term rates than those who believed the market to be in line with their expectations. In any event, only those who have explicit forecasts can decide whether the market is "in line." This is precisely the kind of behavior which I argued above is the central feature of a speculative strategy.

> 5. Investors do appear to exhibit varying degrees of risk aversion in their appraisals of the attractiveness of securities.

Kane and Malkiel found that the investors who found short-term securities relatively attractive differ from the groups who found the market in line, not in their expectations of future long-term rates but rather in the degree of confidence with which they held their expec-tation. Thus, even if the mean expectations were the same, their in-vestors preferred to go short because they were more uncertain of the future. We have not given much weight to differences in the assessment of risk as compared to differences in the assessment of mean returns; but there is no reason why this should be an unimpor-tant factor. Of particular interest is the circumstance that the risk aversion referred to is that of the portfolio managers of the institu-tions: no reference is made to or intended for, the investors who hold the firm's equity. In the next chapter we shall return to the question of whose attitudes toward risk ought to govern.

In sum, this survey evidence suggests that the characterization of subjective risk in Chapter 3 as a situation in which portfolio manag-ers have divergent forecasts of the course of rates and of speculative behavior as based on a manager's awareness of the discrepancy be-tween his own and other forecasts is not far from the mark. Grant-ing this, we have yet to consider the models of interest rate forecast-ing which have been advanced in recent years, though, to be sure, we have seen something of Malkiel's "normal range" hypothesis. Let us turn now to a fuller examination of the work that followed Meiselman's error-learning mechanism.

B. MODELS OF INTEREST RATE FORECASTING

The impact of Meiselman's work has been far-reaching; most investigators coming after him have, like Kessel, followed his lead in adopting the work on distributed lags techniques to the securities market. Meiselman states:

> Recent research in a wide variety of behavioral contexts has indicated that hypothesis which assert that expectations tend to be related to past experience, often a weighted average of past experience, are consistent with the data. Further, these hypotheses state that expectations tend to be systematically altered on the basis of new experience whenever unfolding events differ from what had been anticipated [43, pp. 18-19].[6]

Meiselman's error-learning mechanism is keyed to the second sentence in this quotation; the work to which we now turn is keyed to the first.

Frank Bonello [4] has recently published a very useful study of this forecasting problem. It will be very helpful to make use of his characterization of recent work in the field as well as to review the results of the tests he has made of the various models advanced in this work. He finds that these models of expectations mechanisms can be divided into three categories: regressive, extrapolative, and cyclical which he describes as follows:

> A regressive mechanism is the view that holds that the market expects interest rates to move toward a normal level. The belief that recent changes will lead to further changes is the basic premise for extrapolative mechanisms. Under a cyclical mechanism the hypothesis is that investors take some sort of conceptualization of a normal cyclical rate movement as their expectational guidepost. [4, p. 14][7]

An example of regressive mechanisms is Malkiel's normal range hypothesis referred to just above. Portfolio managers have some notion of the normal range of interest rates and expect rates to move to within that range if, perchance, they happen at any time to be outside it. More generally, if the current level of rates is high (low) relative to the normal level, investors will expect rates to fall (rise). An

---

[6] See Meiselman [43, p. 18] for references to the discussions of distributed lag forecasting models.

[7] It is important to distinguish this use of the term *extrapolative* from the use made of it in Chapter 3. There, extrapolative behavior referred to management behavior when no basis existed for taking speculative positions. It did not refer to the particular way the past data were used to forecast.

extrapolative mechanism is one in which future rate changes are projected as extension of recent rate changes. For a cyclical mechanism, past cyclical movements in rates are expected to be repeated.

More particularly, expectations of future rates can be made in at least three different ways. Under a regressive mechanism the current level of rates is compared to the normal and the difference is used to project future changes in rates. Under an extrapolative mechanism, recent rate changes serve as the basis for projecting future changes. Finally, under a cyclical mechanism both recent changes and levels are used to project future rate changes.

Bonello characterizes these three mechanisms by five equations. He has three for the extrapolative mechanisms because of the special variants that have been developed in that category. These equations follow:

1. The regressive mechanism:[8]

$$(5\text{-}1) \qquad\qquad r_{n,t,t+1} = R_{n,t} + G_n \left(\overline{R}_{n,t} - R_{n,t} \right)$$

where $r_{n,t,t+1}$ is the expected yield to maturity on an n-period security one period hence, $R_{n,t}$ is current yield to maturity on an n-period security, $\overline{R}_{n,t}$ is the normal level of an n-period yield to maturity, and G_n reflect the amount of speed of the adjustment to be made toward normality during the period. If $G = 1$, the entire adjustment is made in one period. $\overline{R}_{n,t}$ is to be derived in some way from past levels of rates.

2. The extrapolative mechanism:[9]

$$(5\text{-}2) \qquad\qquad r_{n,t,t+1} = R_{n,t} + I_n \left(R_{n,t} - \overline{R}^k_{n,t-1} \right)$$

where $r_{n,t,t+1}$ is the expected n-period yield to maturity one period hence, $R_{n,t}$ is the current n-period yield to maturity, $\overline{R}^k_{n,t-1}$ represent recent past levels of the n-period yield to maturity in contrast to a very long past horizon over which the normal level in Eq. 5-1 is defined, and I_n is a speed of adjustment factor. A variety of ways of formulating $\overline{R}^k_{n,t}$ are possible, the k representing, however, the relatively shorter backward time horizon.

3. The error-learning mechanism:[10]

$$(5\text{-}3) \qquad\qquad r_{n,t,t+1} = r_{n,t-1,t+1} + D_n \left(R_{1,t} - r_{1,t-1,t} \right)$$

where the $r_{n,t,t+1}$ and $r_{n,t-1,t+1}$, are the expected yield to maturity to rule in period $t + 1$, the term in parenthesis Meiselman's forecast

[8] Beside Malkiel, some others who have held the view that interest rates regress toward a normal level are Keynes [33, pp. 201–204] J. Robinson [54].

[9] Examples of the use of this kind of forecasting mechanism are D. Farrar [20], and S. Diller [16].

[10] This is, of course, Meiselman's model.

error, and D_n a speed of adjustment factor. Meiselman's model can be seen to be a special case of the extrapolative mechanism.

    4. The combined regressive-extrapolative mechanism:[11]

$$(5\text{-}4) \qquad r_{n,t,t+1} = R_{n,t} + G_n\,(\overline{R}_{n,t} - R_{n,t}) + (R_{n,t} - \overline{R}^k_{n,t-1})$$

where the terms are described under Eqs. 5-1 and 5-2. Again a variety of ways of estimating $\overline{R}_{n,t}$ and $\overline{R}^k_{n,t}$ from past value of the n-period yield to maturity are possible.

    5. The cyclical mechanism:[12]

$$(5\text{-}5) \qquad\qquad r_{n,t,t+1} = R_{n,t} + J_n\,(r^c_{n,t,t+1} - R^c_{n,t})$$

where $r_{n,t,t+1}$ and $R_{n,t}$ are as before, $R^c_{n,t}$ is the reference point in the normal cycle for the n-period rate, $r^c_{n,t,t+1}$, on the normal cycle one period from the reference point, and J_n is a speed of adjustment factor. Normal cycles and reference points for past data can be established in a variety of ways.

    Other mechanisms are possible, but Bonello regards these as an adequate representation of the approaches used by investigators to test hypotheses above the term structure. Further, they represent competing alternatives for which no *a priori* basis can be found to choose one mechanism over another. To choose between them on empirical grounds Bonello used the yield curve for fixed-maturity U. S. Treasury securities published monthly in the *Treasury Bulletin.*[13] He compared the mechanisms to see which gave the best fit for each of five forward rates: the one, three, five, seven, and nine-year forward yields to maturity the $r_{n,t,t+1}$ of Eqs. 5-1 through 5-5.[14]

    Some mention should be made of the way the $\overline{R}_{n,t}$, $\overline{R}^k_{n,t-1}$, $R^c_{n,t}$ and $r^c_{n,t,t+1}$ were specified. Each of these variables was constructed from past data by following in part procedures used by other investigators and also exploring some new ones. The interested reader should consult Bonello [4, pp. 53-56] for the details. All in all, this led to twelve equations, including two inertial ones. These latter were of the form such that in the first the "current n-year forward rate is regressed against the previous period's n-year forward rate,

---

[11] F. De Leeuw [14] and Modigliani and Sutch [50] have combined extrapolative and regressive elements in this way.

[12] This mechanism is one Bonello developed for, as it were, logical completeness.

[13] "These yield curves are smooth curves fitted by eye to closing quotations. The primary data are formulated by reading off rates for each maturity from these smooth curves" [4, p. 53]. He used quarterly observations even though monthly observations were obtainable. They begin in the third quarter of 1953 and end with the second quarter of 1967.

[14] At each point in time t the problem was to predict what these five different yields would be at time $t + 1$.

while in the second. . . , the current n-year forward rate is regressed against the current n-year rate."[15]

It will be useful to quote from Bonello's conclusion at some length. He states:

> A mechanism can be considered the "correct" mechanism for a particular forward rate if it is the only mechanism free of specification error and consistent with the data. Using correlation and regression analysis and specification error tests in an empirical analysis of the mechanisms including at least one version of each category and two inertia mechanisms indicates that none of the mechanisms tested can be selected as the correct mechanism for the one, three, five, and seven-year forward rates. In each of these instances, there are at least two mechanisms which were free of specification error and consistent with the data. In the case of the nine-year forward rate, all mechanisms except one suffer from specification error. The one mechanism, an extrapolative mechanism in which the recent rate trend is defined as the difference between the current nine-year rate and the previous period's nine-year rate, is also consistent with the data. Consequently, this mechanism is considered the "correct" mechanism for the nine year forward rate.
>
> The empirical results also indicate that four categories of mechanisms—the regressive, the extrapolative, the combined regressive-extrapolative, and the cyclical—all yield high coefficients of determination because each of these mechanisms contains a common independent variable. Indeed when only this variable is used as the sole independent variable, there is no significant loss in explanatory ability. Therefore, although these mechanism categories are conceptually unique, they are not operationally unique. This explains why one investigator, when employing a regressive mechanism, found no differences in his results regardless of how he defined the normal level. It also explains how two similar studies, one employing a regressive mechanism and the other a combined regressive-extrapolative mechanism obtained similar results. [4, p. 72][16]

Thus, Bonello finds that his second inertia mechanism which has only one independent variable, the current n-period yield to maturity, does no worse than any of the other mechanisms. Might not all of these mechanisms be "bootstrap" theories of how expectations are formed?[17] Recall the explanation of how expectations affect security price given in Chapter 3. There it was argued that speculators took positions, or adopted strategies, on the basis of information bearing on supply and demand conditions in future periods, information which led them to believe that the market was "out of

---

[15] See Bonello [4, p. 55].

[16] Bonello refers to Malkiel [38] regarding the seeming lack of significance the definition of normal had for Malkiel's empirical results. The two similar studies are Malkiel [38] and Modigliani and Sutch [50].

[17] See Meiselman [43, p. 31] for a discussion of bootstrapism.

line." If they were right, and the changes in the underlying variables they foresaw became more generally recognized, in due course price and yields conformed to their projections. What is common to all the mechanisms Bonello studied is that they extrapolate from past and current market price data, data available to all at virtually no cost, and the method of extrapolation is virtually the same for all participants. Who, then, attempts to look into the future? To argue, as Meiselman does, that "[t] *he real but statistically unspecified independent variable is unanticipated changes in what the literature would typically call 'the interest rate,'*" [43, p. 31] is to sidestep this question.

How then should the results of regressions in which the level of rates is among the independent variables as well as being the dependent variable be interpreted? As an alternative to the interpretation that the market behaves as if it mechanically extrapolated the past into the future, we may look to the characteristics of the shifts in the underlying variables. Casual inspection of the level of rates from 1951 forward reveals cyclical movement about a rising secular trend. Month to month, and even quarter to quarter changes, are never very great. The slow cyclical movements and even slower secular drift will insure that successive observation of levels will be more nearly of the same magnitude than more distant ones. The serial independence of the long-term series of realized yields reported in the previous chapter can be taken in this context to mean that the best guess of next period's price change is zero so that the best guess of next period's yield to maturity is this period's yield to maturity.[18] It is not surprising then that Bonello's inertial mechanism worked so well.

To argue this interpretation of the lack of serial dependence does not mean that security price changes over a very short period are never very great. Far from it, as the standard deviations of the long-terms reported above attest. It is from these changes that incentives for information processing and speculation arise. Moreover attempts to fit mechanisms of the kind Bonello tested to first difference instead of levels will very likely come to very little, not only because of the lack of serial dependence and great variability in such data but chiefly because to do so would continue to beg the main question. The theory of capital and interest tells us that causation runs from real and policy variables and changes in these variables to security

[18] The cylical movements in the level of rates which produced the positive serial dependence in the short-term realized holding-period yield series noted in Chapter 4 are common knowledge and hence afford no opportunity for speculative profits. The absence of speculative profits is quite consistent with obtaining the commonly expected yield on short-term issues. The period Bonello studied spanned much of the period for which these holding-period yields were observed.

prices. What needs to be explained is the cyclical and secular movements in the underlying variables and also how it is that portfolio managers find it worth their time and energy to attempt to forecast these movements. To reverse the direction of causation and to ignore the substantive issues involved in forecasting is to engage in "bootstrapism."[19]

Extrapolators under the term premium hypothesis do not use extrapolative mechanisms to project interest rates for the purpose of taking speculative positions. Rather, they are portfolio managers holding to the basic portfolio policy designed for those instances when no specific evidence is available to them that the market is "out of line." We will turn to a fuller consideration of base and speculative portfolio policy determination under the term premium hypothesis in the next chapter. But first it may be instructive to see what the data show regarding the magnitude of speculative gains that could accrue to successful speculative strategist. The question is, then, are the possibilities for speculative gains sufficiently attractive to encourage the sustained efforts at information collection and processing assumed by the term premium hypothesis.

One way to calculate the possible returns is to calculate the absolute mean realized holding-period yield on, say, one of the longer than 15-years bond series described in Chapter 4. I have done so and found the absolute mean to be approximately 30 percent per annum whereas the algebraic mean for this series over the same period—from 4/3/58 to 12/28/62, the last three subperiods corresponding more or less to the period Kessel studied—is approximately 1.37 percent per annum. To have achieved such a feat of exceeding the extrapolative (nonforecasting) portfolio policy by 28.63 percent, a portfolio manager must have called all the shots correctly and engaged in a very large volume of weekly transactions. Had he done so and had the stockholders' equity supplied one-tenth of the funds and, say, life insurance policy holders the remaining nine-tenths, and liabilities rolled over without posing special problems as in the example extrapolative management given above, the rate of return to stockholders would have been magnified to 286 percent per annum.[20] Of course, such clairvoyance is unlikely and portfolios cannot be completely rearranged weekly. Nevertheless, a performance one two-hundredth times as good as this would raise the rate of return from 1.37 percent to roughly 2.8 percent for the portfolio and increase the return to shareholders from 13.7 percent to 28.0 percent

[19] See the Appendix to this chapter for a fuller discussion of this question.
[20] See page 103, Chapter 4. Life insurance companies have liabilities in excess of 90 percent of the capital structure.

(neglecting ordinary expenses of operations). Doing somewhat better than chance could pay off if the costs of forecasting are not excessive.[21]

This calculation neglects transactions costs and these are considerable for longer-term securities. However, to question the interpretation of these figures as suggesting that the opportunity cost of not forecasting is 30 percent per annum at the upper limit is to raise the wrong issue. The more cogent question is why are spreads between bid and ask quotations large for long-term securities relative to short-term ones.[22] The answer must be that it is relatively more difficult to forecast the impact of shifts in underlying variables in the distant future; that is, it is inherent in the nonstationarity of system and the immobility of real capital which together determines the character of interest rate risk.

Finally, it may be helpful to take a brief look at one of the widely discussed nonmechanistic techniques for forecasting interest rates.[23] Indeed, the flow of funds technique appears to be the only such approach that can be described in terms of available statistics in a relatively unambiguous way.[24] The purpose of sources and uses of funds analysis is the attempt to find some way to determine whether there will be a gap between the supply of (sources of) funds and the demand (uses) for funds at the current level of rates. We need not review the actual process of forecasting sources and uses, but instead we take note of a class of suppliers which is given special weight in this approach.

The class includes foreigners, individuals, and others; that is, it is a residual category presumed to be highly interest-elastic and which, consequently, acts as a buffer and bellwether. If demand exceeds supply, a rise in the level of rates will lead suppliers in this residual category to step up saving and to run down idle balances. And conversely, an excess supply will cause the funds flow from this sector to diminish as downward pressure on interest rates becomes felt. In practice, one way used to forecast interest rate movements

---

[21] The difficulty of estimating the cost of successful forecasting, where forecasting is not mechanical extrapolation is that what is being forecast is precisely that which is not stable or recurrent. Success then cannot be measured in terms of achieving accuracy with one, 5 and 10 percent confidence limits. What is required is to forecast sufficiently better than chance or that costs are covered when there is no stable revenue function. An extensive study of actual practice going well beyond the survey technique described above may shed some light on these matters.

[22] The spread between bid and ask quotation on a Treasury bond due in ten years is currently about $10; the spread on a Treasury bill due in ten weeks is about $.40.

[23] See, for example, the Salomon Brothers forecast [29].

[24] See [23].

is to treat changes in the supply of funds from the residual category as a leading indicator of interest rate movements.

To the extent that these analysts work with publicly available data, it becomes unclear how this approach can lead to speculative gains. However, "in forecasting the sources and uses statement the experienced analyst initially gets some feel for the magnitude of this *ex ante* gap between supply and demand" [23, p. 237]. What is crucial for our purposes is that a number of institutions do devote resources to attempting to forecast the effects of the behavior of real variables in the system. They may very well take their own advice before they publish it, so that their efforts do in fact correspond to the account of speculative behavior set forth above. In any event, a casual look at this forecasting activity suggests that much goes on that cannot be described as distributed lag extrapolation of trends in interest rates.

APPENDIX TO CHAPTER 5

The reliance of term structure theorists on mechanistic approaches to forecasting is something of a paradox inasmuch as the mechanisms proposed rule out consideration of the principal variables that the received theory of capital and interest suggest are relevant to the management of portfolios. In this book every effort has been made to keep these variables in the forefront of the discussion. One consequence of this has been a very stylized presentation of the term structure with almost no consideration of the historical record of actual term structures. This may seem paradoxical since in Chapter 4, the point was made explicitly in connection with the discussion of the Pareto-Levy distributions and nonstationarity, that the problem of explaining time series behavior of security prices was a historical or autobiographical problem rather than one in which the behavior to be explained is repetitive as comparative static analysis tends to suggest.

In contrast to this approach as a historical treatment, the first chapter of Malkiel's book contains an extensive discussion of historical patterns of term structures, including elaborate three dimensional depictions of term structures covering a 65 year period.[25] How are we to account for this attention to historical detail among those relying so heavily on comparative static analysis and the dearth of it in this book? The answer can, I think, be found

[25] Kessel [32] also gives a great deal of weight to the historical record, including specially constructed displays designed to reveal regularities in cyclical behavior. See also Malkiel [39].

by considering the use investigators such as Malkiel make of this review of the historical data.

Malkiel uses his historical survey to establish "the desiderata a theory of the term structure of interest rates should fulfill" [38, p. 16]. These desiderata turn out to be five features of the historical record which Malkiel believes capture the principal behavioral elements satisfactory theory must explain. These are: (1) the greater volatility of short-term rates; (2) the tendency for descending yield curves to be at higher levels than ascending levels; (3) the presence of the "shoulder" that makes, as it were, the curve flatten out as term to maturity increases; (4) the fact that, on average, short-term rates have been lower than long-term rates over the current century; and (5) the circumstance that the very short-term portion of the yield curve is positively sloped whether the remainder is ascending or descending. Malkiel's normal range hypothesis (described above in this chapter) can be seen as an attempt to develop a model of portfolio management behavior of sufficient generality to show that what happened could have happened because portfolio manager forecasted interest rates in a particular way. Thus, the historical record and the liquidity preference hypothesis, which accords a role to both expectations and risk aversion, can be nicely wedded.

But this is not an explanation of the historical record. Rather, it eliminates the need for a historical explanation of the movements in the underlying variables that ought to have a direct impact on portfolio behavior by making the phenomena studied appear to have been generated by a steady-state process. Here, then, is how this paradox can be unraveled. Those who, like Malkiel, make much of the historical record really reduce history to a repetitive process. If this record is to be treated as a historical process, it is essential that this kind of mechanistic reduction be avoided. The movement of the real variables—productively, thrift, technology, population, tastes—and policy variables over this century are much too complex and extensive to be comprehended in a short treatment of the term structure of interest rates. It is, of course, useful to review the historical record and Malkiel's charts are very useful devices for this purpose. Such a review ought to suggest the complexity of any undertaking which attempts to explain the time paths of the underlying variables that economic theory tells us determine the level and structure of interest rates.

chapter 6

On Portfolio Management Policies of Financial Intermediaries

Term structure theorists have not often developed models of institutional portfolio policy that go beyond the notion of the selection of asset maturities according to the specifications of a preferred habitat. Indeed, for most writers speculation is defined as a departure from this habitat. In this approach the question of how hedging behavior maximized the present value of shareholder's equity was not raised. We shall take this present value maximization as a first approximation to the objectives of rational management, portfolio or otherwise. The use of the term "portfolio manager" to refer to both individual and institutional situations also covers over this question of how shareholder attitudes toward risk influence institutional risk taking. This difficulty was alluded to at the end of Chapter 3, and it is now time to confront it directly.

I shall proceed by first showing that there is ample precedent for treating financial intermediaries as though they were households possessed of utility functions of the kind described in Chapter 3. The next step will be to show that in the static equilibrium case, an institutional utility function is not only desirable, but necessary if intermediaries are to have determinate asset and liability structures. I will then show why this static framework cannot adequately characterize what is involved in the management of institutional portfolios. Finally we will close with a review of some empirical work bearing on the base, or nonspeculative, portfolio policies of financial intermediaries.

A. THE NOTION OF AN INSTITUTIONAL UTILITY FUNCTION

Nonhedging pressure models of portfolio selection in financial intermediaries have figured in a wide range of studies of financial and monetary questions. However, for the most part, these studies have been concerned with the problems that touched on selected aspects of institutional portfolio policy. They did not focus directly on institutional portfolio policy as such. Consequently, general treatments of portfolio policy in financial intermediaries are not plentiful. Whatever their shortcomings, these specialized models provide a useful point of departure from which to develop a theory of intermediary policy, which covers default free and risky asset selection and management under both stationary and nonstationary conditions.

In one way or another, these models posit institutional utility functions which, like household utility functions, govern risk-bearing behavior. A common form of institutional preference is to be found in the notion of a desired free reserve position developed in money supply analysis.[1] A careful look at one such model of institutional risk preferences will serve to show how the utility analysis for individuals developed above can be adapted for the analysis institutional choice.

M. Polakoff [53] developed a model of institutional risk preferences to explain commercial bank borrowing from the Federal Reserve System which is formally quite similar to the Markowitz and Sharpe models of individual portfolio choice described above. Polakoff sought to reconcile two views of why banks borrowed from the Fed; namely,

> (a) that they borrow because of profit considerations at such times as they can find outlets for additional funds at market rates of interest higher than the discount rate and (b) that they borrow out of 'need,' i.e., that they do not borrow to re-lend at a profit but rather resort to the discount window to meet adverse clearing balances and the temporary loan demands of their customers and that they repay these debts as quickly as possible. [53, pp. 1-2]

We shall be concerned here less with the substantive issues involved in these two views and more with the formal analysis Polakoff developed to reconcile them.

Polakoff goes on to say that "assuming both motives to be significant, one should be able to analyze the behavior of member banks in terms of utility functions and indifference curves." The model is depicted in Fig. 6-1. The vertical axis represents total bank earnings or profits, the horizontal axis the volume of borrowing from the Fed.

---

[1] See, for example, Meigs [42] and also DePrano [15].

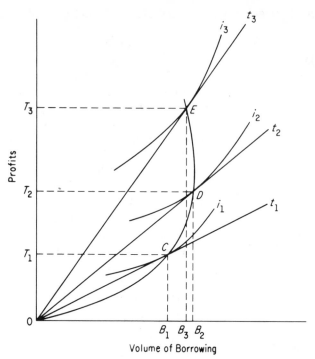

Fig. 6-1. Polakoff's model of bank borrowing.
i_1, i_2, i_3 represent the bank's preferences. $0t_1$,
$0t_2$, and $0t_3$ represent alternative relationships
between borrowing and profits.

The thrust of the model is to show how, even though profits rise with borrowing, utility need not do so. Point C represents the level of profits T_1 associated with the volume of borrowing B_1 when the difference between the rate at which the bank can lend and the rate at which it can borrow from the Fed—the least cost spread—is a positive amount, t_1.[2] The ray from the origin $0t_1$ shows a linear relationship between profits and borrowing on the assumption that bank lending and borrowing are independent of the actions of the individual bank. The greater the spread—suppose $t_1 < t_2 < t_3$—the steeper the slope of ray from the origin.

The form of the indifference curves i_1, i_2 and i_3 reflect both the profit motive—profits are desirable and hence utility increases as profits increase with borrowings held constant—and the need motive

[2] The least cost spread is the difference between, say the ninety-day bill rate and the discount rate established by the Federal Reserve. Since the latter rate is directly under the control of the authorities, the spread can be manipulated as a policy tool.

—borrowings are undesirable and hence utility decreases as borrowings increase with profits held constant. Moreover, the disutility of
borrowing increases as the level of profits increases, imparting to the
indifference curves a special form which leads to the backward bending expansion path, curve $OCDE$. This means that as the least cost
spread increases, the volume of borrowing first increases as the profit
motive dominates but later decreases as the reluctance of banks to be
indebted to the Federal Reserve becomes dominant, as represented
by the curve $OCDE$.

The notion of an expansion path is to be regarded here as a locus
of points consistent with an alternative least cost spread and bank
preferences at a given point in time. The expansion path resembles a
conventional supply schedule, in this instance a supply of bank debt
curve, the inverse of a demand for loanable funds' schedule for an
individual bank. We may therefore conclude that we are still within
the static equilibrium framework in which the utility analysis set
forth in Chapter 3 was based.

Utility functions of the kind usually employed in the portfolio
balance approach would not produce indifference maps with characteristics leading to a backward bending supply of debt scheduled. In
the usual analysis, this supply curve displays everywhere a positive
elasticity reflecting the fact that profits provide utility and borrowing which entails risk brings with it disutility. As we shall see, utility
functions of the usual kind imply that, for the risk averting portfolio
holders, sufficiently large increments of return will induce holders to
bear associated increments of risk. The evidence is crucial here:
special cases such as this one may correspond to the facts. However,
the evidence Polakoff presented did not support a backward bending
expansion path.[3]

By using the formal structure derived from considerations of
household decisions concerning the bearing of risk and applying it to
a firm, Polakoff implicitly assumed an institutional utility function.
Of course, Polakoff's analysis does not confront risk, especially interest rate risk, in a direct way. Instead of risk aversion he uses the notion of reluctance to get the indifference curve to reflect the risk-
return trade-off implied by risk aversion. What is of particular
interest to us here is that by changing Polakoff's model to accord

[3] Polakoff's tests involve time series analysis of the banking system as a
whole. Thus, he attempts to observe the expansion path over time rather than
estimating its parameters at a point in time. While he finds a backward bending
curve, this result is probably best interpreted as a result of nonstationarity. Almost all the observations of the backward bending portion are from the same
recessionary period. See [53, pp. 12-16] especially Chart IVB, which contains
these observations.

with standard utility theory we can move from a model concerned with only one aspect of intermediary portfolio behavior to a comprehensive model of intermediary portfolio choices under static conditions.

We can analyze bank borrowing behavior by positing institutional utility functions of the kind which yield indifference curves in the same variables, expected yield and risk, as used to describe household indifference curves. Figure 6-2 depicts Polakoff's bank borrowing problem with indifference curves in these variables derived, as it were, from the bank's utility function and a linear efficient opportunity set. The bank seeks to produce a common stock with expected yield $\hat{r}_s$ and risk, σ_{r_s} at point s. It achieves this by holding assets with the yield and risk characteristics $\hat{r}_a$ and σ_{r_a}, at points which, because of borrowing in the form demand and time deposits, produce the net stockholder position given by point s.[4]

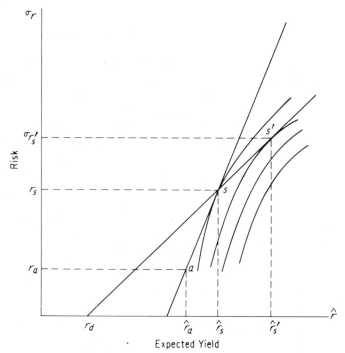

Fig. 6-2. Polakoff's case in the portfolio balance framework.

[4] For convenience we may assume that the bank can borrow at the riskless rate, r_p. As we saw in Chapter 3, borrowing at the riskless rate leads to a linear extension of the opportunity set. See the discussion on pages 62-63.

Now suppose the Federal Reserve permits borrowing at a discount rate $r_d < r_p$. This has the effect of pivoting the bank's efficient opportunity set through r_d and s so that by borrowing from the Fed the bank can produce common stock which offers both a higher expected yield, $\hat{r}_{s'}$, and a higher risk $\sigma_{r_{s'}}$, and also higher utility at s' as seen by the portfolio manager who interprets the bank's utility function. As long as the indifference curves are regular—that is, do not have special features as depicted in Fig. 6-1—increases in the least cost spread $r_p - r_d$ will lead to increased but not unlimited borrowing.[5] Thus we have a model which accounts for asset and liabilities positions in terms of the characteristics of the firm's common stock and for institutional response to changes in one aspect of its environment. Thus, s and s' in Fig. 6-2 are the basic portfolio positions taken by portfolio managers when they have no special information to justify taking speculative positions, which is to say, when they extrapolate the past into the future. What remains is to establish the legitimacy of imputing utility functions to institutions.

B. INSTITUTIONAL UTILITY FUNCTION AND PRESENT VALUE MAXIMIZATION

In the more traditional theory of the firm, maximization of profit, or alternatively, of the market value of the firm's equity, provides sufficient guidance for managerial decisions. If investors' attitudes toward risk, together with the basic risk characteristics of assets, determine the structure of yields on financial assets and hence the price of the firm's equity, how can institutional utility functions of the kind just attributed to financial intermediaries affect portfolio decisions without impairing the sovereignty of investors' preferences? Put differently, in what sense is it legitimate to apply elements of the theory of household behavior to the behavior of firms? To answer these questions it will be helpful to review the now famous Modigliani-Miller (MM) propositions about the independence of the market value of the firm's equity from its liability structure.[6] Their line of reasoning can readily be extended to include asset structures and to the general equilibrium case. Consequently, we will be able to show that institutional utility functions are entirely consistent with traditional profit maximization.

[5] It should be emphasized that this is a comparative static analysis in which successive equilibria are compared. We neglect at this point the problem of managing in an environment of continual disequilibrium but return to it below.

[6] See F. Modigliani and M. H. Miller [49]. This paper can also be found in S. Archer and C. D'Ambrosio [1] together with a number of commentaries on it and replies by MM.

Early work in a problem area often results in special solutions which help make possible more general solutions later. The MM model is no exception to this rule. It is a partial equilibrium analysis of the effects of borrowing and lending on portfolio opportunities open to households. The situation is represented in Fig. 6-3 by point q in the interior of the opportunity set. The efficient opportunity set, represented by the line through r_p and point a, depicts the Sharpe general equilibrium market line with homogeneous expectations. Point q, then, shows the expected yield and risk characteristics of firms in industry Q which are entirely financed by their shareholders; that is, the firms have not borrowed. We may now investigate the question MM raised; namely, what would be the impact on the expected yield and risk of a firm in industry Q if it substituted debt for equity in its capital structure.[7] For the moment we ignore the effect of income taxes, returning to the problems they pose shortly.

The MM propositions can be represented by the line through r_p and q for essentially the same reason the efficient boundary is linear under Sharpe's assumption of riskless lending and borrowing.[8] However, MM did not take this tack. Instead they argued that, for example, if the shares of a levered firm (one which is partly financed by debt) sold at a yield $\hat{r}_{q'}$, given by q' in Fig. 6-3, arbitrageurs would sell the shares of such firms, buy those of an unlevered firm in the industry, financing themselves in part by borrowing on their own account.[9] In doing this, they could achieve a net-expected yield and risk position on their own levered portfolios on the linear extension r_p through q represented by q'' in Fig. 6-3. In the process they would have brought down the price of the shares of levered firms such that their yields would also be $\hat{r}_{q''}$. This possibility of home-made leverage will ensure that the market value of the firm remains constant by ensuring that increases in yields resulting from corporate borrowing are just sufficient to offset risk with the consequence that share prices are invariant with respect to leverage. Standard prescriptions of rational management specifying the maximization of

[7] Replacing equity with debt in this context is a conceptual experiment formally equivalent to the riskless borrowing assumed by Sharpe. See the discussion in Chapter 3, pages 62-63.

[8] In the MM diagram, risk is measured by the ratio of debt to equity rather than by the dispersion of possible yields. However, since MM posit such a dispersion the σ_r measure is implicit in their analysis.

[9] This arbitrage argument parallels closely Meiselman's notion of how speculators make the term structure reflect their expectations. The difference is the minor one that MM assume risk aversion and Meiselman assumes indifference to risk. In both instances static equilibrium is assumed.

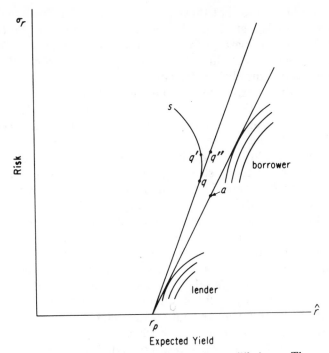

Fig. 6-3. Portfolio opportunities in equilibrium. The
Modigliani and Miller model in the Sharpe framework.

share price will not therefore provide guidance for corporate borrowing under the static equilibrium conditions assumed here.

The result that leverage does not affect market value of shares
has been the object of considerable criticism, much of it aimed at
showing that in the "real" world there is some optimum level of
corporate borrowing that maximizes the market value of the firm.[10]
Central to most of this criticism is the argument that in the real
world, imperfections of various kinds—imperfect information, divergence of views, high costs of personal (homemade) leverage—mean
that some optimum does exist. The problem with this line of reasoning is that imperfections exist, but that their existence cannot be
handled by minor modification of the static equilibrium solutions.[11]
In terms of the analysis developed in Chapter 3 these imperfections
produce the condition of subjective risk, the possibility of divergent
expectations and consequent opportunity for speculation. What

[10] See, for example, D. Durand [18]; also in [1].
[11] Such an optimum implies a stable backward bending curve depicted in
Fig. 6-3 as the ray $r_p qs$.

ought to be argued is that these imperfections might well give rise to optimal speculative strategies.[12]   As in the argument presented in Chapter 3, there is hardly any need for managers in the stationary state. For the moment, however, it will be useful to continue with the Sharpe static equilibrium framework.

Since neither corporate nor personal income taxes preclude a static equilibrium, the effect of such taxes can properly be considered in the present context. Interest payments reduce corporate tax liabilities so that in the absence of personal income taxes, maximizing firms would have a clear incentive to completely replace equity with debt. Legal restraints prevent such extreme behavior but do not prevent substantial debt financing. However, given personal income tax, this profit incentive for corporate borrowing would depend on the marginal tax rate of shareholders and the opportunities they have for "homemade" leverage. Since the marginal tax rates of shareholders are not fixed, and since shareholders can shift among firms, shares could come to fall in the hands of shareholders for whom the tax shield offered by corporate debt just offset the tax shield relinquished by relying on corporate rather than personal borrowing.[13]   In this way the initial invariance of market value with respect to leverage would be reestablished.

If, then, the level of corporate borrowing is indeterminate with respect to the maximization rule, it follows that the risk associated with the firm's equity cannot be directly linked to household preferences. Indirectly the attitudes of investors do have their influence—their attitudes are a major factor in determining the slope of the efficient set. Nevertheless, a degree of indeterminacy does exist with respect to liability structures which, for a financial intermediary, could be eliminated by the existence of institutional preferences for liability structures. It remains to be shown that this indeterminacy exists as well for asset structures.

To extend the MM argument to include the risk characteristics of the firm's assets as subject to institutional preferences, we need only note that households can offset the asset choices of managers by appropriate shifts in the asset composition of their own portfolios. The possibility of "homemade" diversification—the counterpart to "homemade" leverage—breaks the link between households' attitudes towards risk and the firm's asset structure. In the absence of such a link, it would appear that the risk aspects of portfolio decisions in

[12] See MM in [11, p. 155] for a discussion of strategies.
[13] What is crucial here are the differentials between corporate and personal income tax rates and the proportion of shareholders in different tax brackets. The matching of shareholders to firms assumed in the text is an oversimplification of a very complex question.

large publicly held financial intermediaries cannot be explained by the direct influence of household preferences. However, as with the clientele effect that taxes may produce, departures from established portfolio policies can entail cost for investors and hence could be governed by profit considerations. However, determination of initial policies cannot be handled in this way, thus leaving a basic indeterminacy.

Having seen that some kind of mechanism internal to the firm is necessary to determine portfolio policy—or more broadly, to permit decisions about the bearing of risk and uncertainty—we turn to a consideration of some specific hypotheses about institutional utility functions. It will be useful to begin with a consideration of some of the recent developments in the theory of the firm.

C. INSTITUTIONAL UTILITY FUNCTIONS: THEORIES AND EVIDENCE

A number of theories proposing the possibility of departures from strict profit or present value maximizing rules have appeared in the last decade.[14]   Management goals in these theories include reve- nue maximization subject to minimum profit constraints; satisfaction of performance targets for profits, sales, and other variables, at levels which are determined by past experience of aspirations and achieved satisfactions; and maximization of managerial utility functions which contain as arguments certain variables that preclude strict profit maximization. In each of these instances, the pursuit of these goals depends on the slack provided by the lack of vigorous competition in the product markets and also upon the existence of uncertainty which makes information costly and often available only with a lag.

Because we are concerned for the present with a static equilib- rium case in which information is essentially a free good—all the relevant probability distributions are known by all participants—and competition in financial markets is rigorous, these theories do not offer much help in formulating models of portfolio choice in finan- cial intermediaries. Indeed, it is precisely the need for managerial discretion in the absence of all slack, that provides a major point of departure from the received theory of the firm in the present analy- sis. However, once we turn to the problems associated with non- stationarity, certain portions of these behavioral theories will prove useful. In particular, variables cited by O. Williamson such as mana- gerial desires for empire building and control over investment deci-

---

[14] A useful discussion of these theories can be found in K. Cohen and R. Cyert [11].

sions will give added dimensions to the discretion they already possess to determine the risklessness of the firm's assets and liability structures [68].

In view of the dearth of suggestions in the recent literature on behavioral theories of the firm applicable to the static equilibrium case under perfect competition, let us turn to the notion of the institutional utility function. This function affords the means to bring the determination of the risk characteristics of the various asset and liability items of intermediaries into a single decision framework. In terms of Fig. 6-2, once the point s is found at which an indifference curve derived from an intermediary's utility function is tangent to efficient opportunity set, the intermediary selects a portfolio of assets, say $\hat{r}_a$, σ_{r_a} at a and issues liabilities in a sufficient amount so that the impact of asset and liability decisions transforms the asset yield and risk characteristics into the net equity characteristics, $\hat{r}_s$, σ_{r_s}. Maximization in the usual sense consists in getting to the efficient set though, of course, it excludes selection of the particular point in the set. How does this utility function arise?

On one level, not the most fundamental, we may say that managerial attitudes towards risk must be among the factors having a significant influence on institutional utility functions. See in this way, the notion of an institutional utility function draws attention to the institutional process—institutional in the sense of being outside the usual maximization considerations but nonetheless not irrational—that produce portfolio policies. What is crucial here is that rational behavior, the maximization of profits or of present values, can only be defined once policy objectives have been determined. The process of policy determination deserves a much more central place in the discussion of portfolio management than it has hitherto received. Often the policy determination process is treated as a kind of institutional practice which impedes or severely constrains attempts at maximization.[15]   It is only in static equilibrium context, one in which novelty and uncertainty are ruled out, that irrationality can be rigorously defined. Thus, in Sharpe's model, it would be irrational to hold a portfolio characterized by a point not on the boundary. In the nonstationary context in which institutional practices are actually observed it is exceedingly difficult to specify concretely what irrationality is. We shall return to this point below.

[15] For example, it has been argued that market segmentation arises as the consequence of institutional practices. Critics of the segmented market hypothesis see such arguments as implying widespread irrationality since, in absence of such impediments, movement between maturities must occur since such movement would be entailed by profit maximization.

One hypothesis that provides the beginning of an explanation of the institutional utility function is that it is the characteristics of the liabilities that give rise to the particular characteristics on a firm's utility function so that firms in a given industry tend to have similar functions. Another way of saying this is that institutional practices are industry practices. Financial industries are usually identified by the ways the firms they comprise raise borrowed funds.[16] Thus, common patterns of liability and asset structures may result from the way important nonrational factors make their influence felt.[17] To anticipate some of the evidence to be reviewed shortly, to be a fire and casualty insurance underwriter is to be committed to offering common stock with certain well-understood risk characteristics. Policies of this kind would lead households to regard intermediaries as providers of diversification services. In a static equilibrium context the decision to be a certain kind of diversified fund is simply not a maximizing one in the usual sense.

As was argued in Chapter 3, in the static equilibrium case information is essentially a free good. Diversification services make sense only in a world where information collection and processing is costly and where continuous monitoring is necessary. In a word, the existence of a wide range of diversified funds specializing in different kinds of assets and offering different kinds of diversified portfolios makes sense only in a nonstationary context. It is important to keep this in mind in reviewing the following evidence.

Evidence bearing on this industry-wide utility function hypothesis is rather skimpy. Perhaps the most suggestive is that presented by J. Michaelsen and R. Goshay in their study of fire and casualty underwriters [46]. They advanced the hypothesis that stock fire and casualty firms aim at producing common stock with similar risk and return characteristics. To test this hypothesis directly would require estimates of expected yield and risk characteristics, which as we have seen in connection with the test of the expectations hypothesis, are exceedingly difficult to come by, especially estimates of expected yield. Moreover, the notion of a single expected yield common to the market precludes the nonstationarity which is the principal justification for the existence of financial intermediaries. What Michaelsen and Goshay did was to construct proxies for expected yield and risk from balance sheet ratios such as the ratio of common stock to

[16] One exception is mutual funds, though mutual funds can be classed according to specifically stated policy objectives. See D. Farrar [20] for discussion of mutual fund policies and behavior.

[17] A full account of how policy objectives come to be reached is beyond the scope of this study. It would involve political, social and psychological as well as historical analyses. However, see M. Grove [26].

bonds as a measure of asset risk and underwriting liabilities to stock-holder equity as a measure of liability risk.[18]   In one sense these measures are preferable to measure involving security prices directly such as those discussed in Chapter 5 because these balance sheet ratios can be taken as base portfolio positions from which speculative positions are taken and thus bear on behavior in a nonstationary context. In a nonstationary context there can be no stable measure of either risk or expected yield.

Following the logic of the "homemade" diversification argument outlined above, the risk on the equity depends on both asset and liability structures jointly.   If asset risk is relatively high (a relatively large ratio of common stock to bonds), a given yield-risk objective can be reached by a relatively safe liability structure (a relatively small ratio of underwriting to shareholder equity).   Thus, if firms in an industry do aim at the same risk objectives for the equity we should observe that firms with risky asset structures have relatively safe liability structures and conversely, relatively safe asset structures should be associated with risky liability structures. In cross sections of large stock fire and casualty firms for each of four years Michaelsen and Goshay found strong inverse correlation between these asset and liability risk indexes of the kind predicted by the hypothesis.

Michaelsen and Goshay also presented results for samples of mutual underwriters.   Correlation between the asset and liability risk indexes was significant but less strong for the mutual samples. While further investigation is necessary to reach firm conclusions about the greater divergence of behavior among mutuals, this divergence suggests that the absence of equity in the usual sense is a matter of some consequence even though institutional forces that appear to be at work in the stock companies seem to be also in mutual companies. Portfolio selection when the maximization rules have no clear-cut reference to specific equity value is a fascinating problem, but one which cannot be pursued here.   The point to be stressed is that the notion of an institutional utility function arising in a context of a financial industry appears to be consistent with a first look at some relevant data.

Other evidence on institutional utility functions was provided by Carson and Scott in their study of commercial bank balance sheets similar in certain respects to the study just discussed [9].   Commercial banks play a much more central role in the monetary system

---

[18] The ratio of common stock to bonds in the asset holding is a crude measure of asset risk since there can be much variation among the individual issues in each category.   The ratio of underwriting liabilities to shareholder's equity is less subject to this difficulty.

than fire and casualty underwriters. Evidence on how they decide overall portfolio policy would be of considerably more interest in understanding the linkages by which the monetary authority influences policy targets. Unfortunately, because commercial banks are a much more heterogeneous collection of firms—the fire and casualty firms participate in nationwide asset and liability markets whereas banks do not—the regression analysis is more difficult to interpret. Nevertheless, the Carson and Scott findings are worth reviewing for they do provide support for industry-wide hypothesis.

Carson and Scott sought to examine the influence of selected commercial bank attributes (size, rate of growth, ratio of time to total deposits, ratio of capital to total deposits) on the "willingness of these banks to bear risk." Thus, some of the independent variables in the regression analysis correspond to the indexes of liability structure risk used in the Michaelsen-Goshay study. The dependent variable— "the degree of risk aversion"—was measured by alternative asset ratios none of which were designed to reflect the overall characteristics of the asset structure.[19] More important, Carson and Scott conceived the liability characteristics as "causing" the asset characteristics, rather than the two kinds of characteristics jointly "causing" the equity characteristics. However, the regression analysis itself can be interpreted as revealing the jointness rather than causation even though the asset risk measures reflect only limited aspects of the asset structure.

The asset ratios that included the largest proportion of the asset structure that Carson and Scott used were the ratio of cash reserves and Treasury securities to total assets and the ratio of net loans and discounts to total assets. Both of these asset ratios were significantly related to the ratio of time to total deposits in the manner suggested by the industry-wide utility function hypotheses: the greater the proportion of time to total deposits (the less risky the liability structure), the lower the proportion of liquid assets and the higher the proportion of loans in total assets (the more risky the asset structure). The total variance explained was lower in this than in the Michaelsen-Goshay study.[20] For the present, we may conclude that

[19] In the regressions Michaelsen and Goshay ran, all asset and liability categories were taken into account whereas the Carson and Scott regressions never included all the balance sheet data at one time. For example, when government securities were in the dependent variable, loan categories were left out of account. This oversight may well have been due to the circumstance that Carson and Scott did not have a comprehensive theory of portfolio management.

[20] The multiple correlation coefficients for Carson and Scott were in most instance less than .5 whereas Michaelsen and Goshay obtained closer to .7 and above.

the notion of an industry-generated institutional utility function is worth further exploration.

The interpretation placed on the findings just reviewed goes beyond the initial problem created by the logical necessity of imputing utility functions to financial intermediaries to explain how, in a static equilibrium context, risk-bearing decisions come to be made. What has been done is to show that industry-wide policy objectives appear to guide portfolio behavior in a way that can be regarded as providing the base portfolio position, departures from which are dictated by speculative strategies.[21] These rules of thumb, as it were, act as signals to households about how the institutions will deal with the risk attendant on nonstationarity. Before turning to some evidence bearing directly on the maturity policies of financial intermediaries it may be helpful to review briefly some work which inadvertently lends additional support to this reading of these findings.

In his classic paper setting forth the portfolio balance approach to the demand for money, James Tobin used a model of portfolio choice which lends itself more directly than does Sharpe's, which was a lineal descendant of Tobin's, to showing why nonstationarity is at the center of interest rate risk.[22] Tobin's purpose in proposing that money be treated as another asset in the context of portfolio management under uncertainty was to remedy what he regarded as a serious shortcoming in the Keynesian liquidity preference theory of the demand for money. In a fundamental sense, nonstationarity is at the center of the Keynesian model and it is precisely this characteristic that Tobin eliminated with his portfolio balance approach.

In the Keynesian theory, the demand for cash stems from those investors who regard the current rate of interest below the "normal" level to which they expect it to return. This impending shift will produce capital losses on bonds, in this case perpetuities or consols, which can be avoided by holding cash instead of consols. Similarly, investors will hold consols when they do not expect a rise in rates or expect them to fall. Thus, this theory of the demand for money depends crucially on divergent expectations whereas the portfolio balance theory does not. It is interesting to note that divergent views here seem to require divergent notions of the "normal" level of rates.

---

[21] It is important to recall that the data used in these regressions were not expectational. These balance sheet ratios would, in regressions, tend to reflect base policies rather than speculative positions. However, they need not be regarded as reflecting static equilibrium positions. Rather, they can be taken as representing working arrangements which change slowly.

[22] See J. Tobin [65]. Sharpe acknowledges his debt to both Tobin and Markowitz [59, p. 476].

Since the past history of rates is a matter of public record, there is some question as to how this divergence arises.[23]

Whatever the cause of the initial divergence, some investors will hold consols and some will hold cash at any given level of interest rates. As the rate falls, it becomes below "normal" for an ever increasing number of investors who prefer cash to the bearing of capital losses. What Tobin sought to do was to devise a means whereby all investors would hold both cash and consols. He did this by making the demand for cash depend on an expected level of rates and the dispersion of possible levels about this expected or mean level. In Fig. 6-4, the vertical axis represents the dispersion of possible future rates about their mean and the horizontal axis the expected rate on consols. Cash offers no explicit yield so that the efficient opportunity set is represented by the ray OC, beginning at an expected yield of

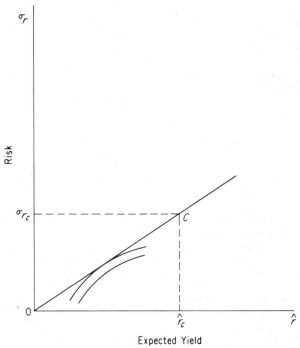

Expected Yield

Fig. 6-4. Tobin's portfolio balance model of the demand for money. Point C represents the characteristics of a default-free consol.

[23] We have already noted the difficulty of the notion of a "normal" level of rates in Malkiel's work in Chapter 5. Perhaps it would be better to assume divergence of expectations without an explanation of why it exists.

zero and extending through point C, representing the characteristics of the consol. As with Sharpe, risk-averting investors will find a point of tangency on the efficient set such that they will hold both cash and bonds. Thus, Tobin eliminated both the all-cash and all-consol investor and with it all divergence of expectations.

However, a number of difficulties arise when divergence of views is eliminated. Consider that under the Keynesian liquidity preference theory as time passes, the divergent expectations will not all prove correct. For example, either rates rise and capital losses are incurred, or they do not rise and hence no capital losses will be realized. Tobin took note of Leontief's criticism that in equilibrium the demand for speculative money balances must be zero since it depended on a divergence between current and expected rates which is bound to vanish as investors learn from experience; no matter how low an interest rate may be, it can be accepted as "normal" if it persists long enough.[24] However, in a nonstationary environment and with an extrapolative mechanism that makes all market participants have the same notion of the "normal" level of rates, the demand for cash will not vanish. Of course, neither will it be stable over time.[25] The question then arises whether nonstationarity is a requirement for a non-vanishing portfolio balance demand for cash.

Tobin then had this to say about his own theory of liquidity preference:

> The risk aversion theory of liquidity preference mitigates the major logical objections to which .. the Keynesian theory is vulnerable. But it cannot completely meet Leontief's position that in a strict stationary equilibrium liquidity preference must be zero unless cash and consols bear equal rates. By their very nature consols and, to a lesser degree, all time obligations contain a potential for capital gain or loss that cash and other demand obligations lack. Presumably, however, there is some length of experience of constancy in the interest rate that would teach the most stubbornly timid investor to ignore that potential. In a pure stationary-state, it could be argued, the interest rate on consols would have been the same for so long that investors would unanimously estimate σ_g [the same index of risk as in Fig. 6-4] to be zero. So stationary a state is of very little interest. Fortunately, the usefulness of comparative statics does not appear to be confined to comparisons of states each of which would take a generation or more to achieve. As compared to the Keynesian theory of liquidity preference, the risk aversion theory widens the applicability of comparative statics in aggregative analysis; this is all that need be claimed for it. [65, p. 85]

It is important to note that the dispersion in Sharpe's model can

[24] See Tobin [65, p. 85].
[25] The reason for this is that nonstationarity will lead to continual change in what is considered normal, unless of course there is no secular drift in the level of rates. This is highly unlikely.

continue over time: learning would not change anything since this dispersion is like the noise in a steady-state system.[26]   However, the same cannot be said for the dispersion in Tobin's model. To keep interest rate risk from vanishing (that is, to keep estimates of Tobin's σ_g from declining to zero) disturbances must occur which disrupt the learning process. The applicability of comparative statics in aggregative analysis along Tobin's lines—which is to say, the extent to which the demand for money function can be regarded as stable—will depend, in part, on such empirical questions as the magnitude and frequency of such disruptions and the character of the learning process. There is no reason why, as an empirical matter, the interaction between disruptions and the learning process should produce estimates of σ_g which remain stable over time. Indeed, it would appear that the characterization of the findings on fire and casualty and commercial bank portfolio practices and base policies in a nonstationary context makes a good deal of sense.

In a recent study [63] W. T. Terrell and W. J. Frazer, Jr. reported findings which lend further support to the industry-wide utility function hypothesis.[27]   Terrell and Frazer studied the maturity distribution of the marketable public debt in the portfolios of a number of institutional investors over the decade of the sixties. Because of this focus on maturity composition, their work is complimentary to that just reviewed on fire and casualty and commercial bank portfolio policies.[28]   The model of institutional portfolio management they sought to test is something of a mix between the one being advanced here and the preferred habitat model.   Fortunately, their findings nevertheless bear in an interesting way on the industry-wide hypothesis so that a brief review of their work should prove useful.

The model they propose is a loose one; it cannot be expressed readily in mathematical terms. Thus, they state:

> In particular, the approach incorporates a form of neo-Bayesian analysis (i.e., utility analysis with probabilistic weighting schemes) that allows for the following: reliance upon guesses, hunches, learning from the past and analyses of data in making decisions concerning the ac-

[26] M. Friedman, in a recent discussion of the demand for money, adopts a conception of risk quite similar to Sharpe's in which "aggregates are constants but individuals are subject to uncertainty and change. Even the aggregates may change in a stochastic way, provided the mean values do not [22, p. 2]." This precludes the nonstationarity which is at the center of interest risk as defined here.

[27] Also W. T. Terrell [63], Jones [30] and B. Malkiel [38] for discussion of institutional practices.

[28] Some of the variables Carson and Scott used measured maturity composition albeit in a rough way. For example they distinguished between debt due in one year or less and all other government debt. Terrell and Frazer explore this aspect of portfolio management in much greater detail.

quisition and distribution of assets as to various classes; and shaky judgment in the sense of uncertainty (as a probability) and the controversial nature of some decisions especially in group and institutional type environments. [64, p. 8]

Many of the ingredients in this list have been discussed, or are implicit in the discussion of speculative strategies in Chapter 3. Terrell and Frazer do not, however, consider these strategic considerations at length. Rather, in place of an analysis of what is involved in forecasting rate movements, they offer "an equality of foresight" principle. This principle compresses information processing role to a simultaneous response by all buyers and sellers to "certain factors," the term Terrell and Frazer use for changes in the underlying variables which determine the level of rates. Put in the terms developed here, portfolio policies are developed which provide the base asset and liability structures or positions from which portfolio managers attempt to cope with nonstationarity. The equality of foresight principle has the effect of leading Terrell and Frazer to concentrate on what portfolio managers do when they do not have information that the market is "out of line" and to largely ignore speculative behavior.[29]

I do not wish to suggest by this analysis of their use of the equality of foresight principle that Terrell and Frazer ignore speculative behavior out of ignorance. In their view much of the information required for successful speculation is simply not attainable. But much is not all. In my view speculation is a crucial supplement to the approach Terrell and Frazer take to portfolio management. The possibility of speculative profits provides the motive force whereby such information as is attainable on novel circumstances comes to influence security prices. There is no disjunction implied between speculation and managing the base portfolio. What goes on in most financial intermediaries is an admixture of largely more or less routine activity and occasional speculation. It is important to emphasize that what is routine is not mere routine. The cost of maintaining the base position differ sharply from what would be involved in a once for all selection process in a stationary context. In such a world there would be no routine management. Thus, taking a speculative position entails incremental costs to be added on the already considerable cost of "routine" information processing. We may then take the equality of foresight principle as a way of viewing the management of the base portfolio which is much, but far from all, of the story.

What then, is their conception of the institutional utility function

[29] This discussion does not do justice to the Terrell and Frazer, who were concerned in their paper to show that portfolio selection is a special case of economic choice in general. They make a considerable effort to show how their analysis fits into more general choice theory.

and the factors which determine it? They state:

> There are several major conditions likely influencing portfolio selec-
> tion by various groups: (1) uncertainty with respect to some economic
> future common to all; (2) uncertainty with respect to relatively unique
> events and prospects concerning specific groups; and (3) the liability
> structure of the particular groups in question. Uncertainty may be with
> respect to unanticipated and anticipated outlays, receipts, lines of
> credit, and so on. Such analysis suggests an interrelationship between
> portfolios and liabilities and divergent portfolios to deal with specialized
> needs ... and liability structures. Indeed, the portfolios of the groups
> presently studied, including primarily financial institutions, are distin-
> guished especially in terms of their liabilities. [64, p. 10]

This emphasis on significance of the liability structure parallels
that in the industry-wide utility function hypothesis. As will be apparent below, they also give weight to the timing of payments due on
liabilities as consonant with the hedging notion of interest rate risk.
Let us now turn to the findings. Terrell and Frazer's procedure is to
develop a set of criteria for the marketable federal debt in the hands
of eight classes of institutional holders based on the conception of the
determinants of portfolio policy just quoted above. The eight classes
are as follows: commercial banks, mutual savings banks, life insurance
companies, fire and casualty companies, savings and loan associations,
nonfinancial corporations, state and local government general funds,
and state and local government pension and retirement funds. With
the exception of nonfinancial corporations, which are likely to be
quite heterogeneous, the classes correspond reasonably well to the
notion of an industry defined by the characteristics of its liabilities.

The criteria are (1) maturity of expected investment realization,
(2) provision for unanticipated outlays, (3) certainty of return and
marketability of other assets, and (4) homogeneity and/or dates of
anticipated outlay. The concern with the matching of cash inflows
and outflows is clear. Terrell and Frazer then apply these criteria to
the eight classes and deduce systematic differences among them. For
example, they regard banks and nonfinancial corporations as desiring
on the average short maturities (criterion 1), mutual savings banks,
life insurance companies and pension and retirement funds as desiring
long maturities, and fire and casualty, savings and loan associations
and general funds as desiring intermediate maturities. What is crucial
for present purposes is that there be significant differences among
classes that show up in data, rather than the particular explanations
given for the differences.

To be sure, whether or not the data is inconsistent, the industry-
wide hypothesis is not a matter of indifference. What is required is a
means of specifying what kinds of behavior would be inconsistent.

At this stage we are largely establishing the empirical regularities which need to be explained. These findings and the ones just reviewed are more suggestive than definitive. For example, since bank loans have extremely poor secondary markets, the burden of marketability falls on the government debt. But, as the Carson and Scott data suggest, the maturity of this debt depends on the ratio of time to total deposits as well as on asset characteristics.[30] Thus, maturity composition is tied to risk and yield characteristics of the institution's equity, and these cannot be determined by maximization rules alone. Consequently, the desire of banks for short-term marketable debts may not be linked the way the Terrell and Frazer criteria suggest.

Given a characterization of the differing policy objectives for marketable debt for the eight groups, Terrell and Frazer, then, translate these differences into implication for the behavior of the data they observed. The data are quarterly maturity distributions for the eight groups mentioned taken from the U. S. Treasury Survey of Ownership during the period March 31, 1960 to June 30, 1969. The survey reports par value holdings for these eight groups and some others for about 65 separate securities ranging from one day to about 30 years' maturity.[31] For each of the eight groups they computed for each quarter the following characteristics of the distribution of its holdings among the various maturities: (1) the variance which tells whether the distribution tends to flatten out more or less; (2) the mean which indicates whether the distribution is located more in one maturity direction or another; (3) the quartiles which divide the maturity range up into four segments, such that the distribution over the first two quartiles (or the range from zero to the median) accounts for one-half of the debt, and that over the first three quartiles three-quarters of the debt; (4) a coefficient of skewness, such that zero value suggest symmetry, positive values a tailing off to the right; and (5) a coefficient of kurtosis such that its value varies about the number 3 as the distribution from one with more than normal "peakedness" to less.

Before reviewing how the behavior of these computed statistics relate to their hypothesis about institutional portfolio management, it may be helpful to first examine some of the general characteristics of these holdings and Terrell and Frazer's interpretation of them. They found the maturity distributions for the various groups "remarkably stable" over the period. Because this stability occurs over a time during which the level and structure of interest rates changed markedly,

---

[30] See [9, pp. 426-427].

[31] They ignore private debt holdings because data on them is not readily available. This is not a satisfactory solution to this problem though it is an understandable one.

they view this stability as casting some doubt "on the relevance of the received expectations theory of the term structure in two respects: (1) institutions are not indifferent about their maturity profiles; and (2) changes appear in the term structure without concomitant adjustments in the quantities of short-term maturities relative to long-term ones [64, p. 11]."[32]

While this interpretation is consistent with the data, it may go too far. Over the period studied the maturity composition of public debt was not remarkably unstable, though it did vary, rising slightly from 1960 to 1965 and declining somewhat more sharply thereafter.[33] Thus, if the Treasury tailors the debt to meet the "needs" of the market we should not be surprised to find relative of stability of the kind Terrell and Frazer found. It is precisely whether or not to tailor the debt in this way that is at the center of policy issue of principal concern to us here. We shall review the other evidence on the relationship between changes in the maturity composition of the outstanding debt and the term structure in the next chapter. Nevertheless, it does seem clear that factors other than shifts in maturity composition of the outstanding debt such as changes in the underlying variables listed at the end of Chapter 2, can affect security prices without requiring extensive portfolio alterations. Put somewhat differently, a relatively small amount of speculative behavior may go a long way toward making security prices reflect the fundamental factors of productivity, thrift, technological and demographic change and policy actions that economic theory tells us they should.

Turning now to the behavior of the various statistics of the maturity distributions of the eight groups studied, Terrell and Frazer find that not only do the groups differ in average maturity as was described just above, ranging nonfinancial corporations and banks with the shortest maturities to life insurance companies and pension and retirement funds with the longest, but the other statistics are also well-behaved. Thus, as they predicted, when they regressed the higher moments of these distributions on the mean, the standard deviation and mean were directly related, skewness and the mean inversely related, and kurtosis and the mean inversely related.[34] They concluded that "[t]he resulting coefficients provide striking evidence of a fairly

[32] Terrell and Frazer stress the fact that "[m]aintaining profiles of the type we have described actually require transactions as time passes." The need for these transactions reduces the deterrent effect of transaction costs would have on portfolio adjustment and these costs should not, therefore, be given much weight in explaining the stability of maturity profiles.

[33] See Fig. 1 [64, p. 14].

[34] The total sample size was 240 observations: this included eight observations in a cross section and thirty such cross sections.

smooth and temporally stable institutional continuum of maturity profile, and this is in accord with our being able to rank institutions according to their liability structures [64, p. 19]." However, as has already been noted, there are other explanations for this observed empirical regularity and much work remains to distinguish among them.

The problem of distinguishing among alternative models of portfolio management is especially complicated because of the difficulty of specifying what rational or maximizing behavior entails. As we have seen, in a stationary context, portfolio policies lie outside strict profit maximizing considerations, In a nonstationary context portfolio practices are important but the meaning of rationality becomes unclear when it is uncertain what the future holds and hence no way to determine what the "best" policy would be.[35] However, in a nonstationary context actual term structure behavior indicates that it would be profitable in a gross sense for financial intermediaries to have a forecasting capacity and to translate forecasts into portfolio policy. While it appears that, in fact, intermediaries do have some such capacity, whether such translation occurs is an open question. Establishing whether costs of such a capacity are prohibitive is not an easy matter. The behavior Terrell and Frazer observed is not related directly to this question. Thus, most of the work involved in rigorous testing of the alternatives lies ahead.

Before turning to the question of debt management policy it will be useful to summarize the interpretations of the evidence presented in Chapters 4, 5, and 6 as it bears on the question of whether maturity composition of the outstanding debt has an influence on the level and structure of interest rates. How well does the evidence jibe with the term premium hypothesis which, with its associated hypothesis of portfolio management, predict that increases (decreases) in the maturity of the debt outstanding will raise (lower) long rates relative to short ones and may alter the level of all rates as well?

In Chapter 4, Kessel's finding that forward short-term rates systematically overestimated subsequent spot rates—which is logically equivalent to the rising means in Michaelsen's short-term time series of realized yields—suggests the hypothesis that security prices at a point in time are lower than they would be on the basis of expectations alone and that the magnitude of this difference increases with term to maturity. The positive association between the standard deviations of the time series and their term to maturity together with

---

[35] Sharpe's model shows what is involved in the notion of rationality. In the absence of the information required to reach equilibrium in his model, no precise specification of rationality is possible.

the instability of the standard deviations over time and their relatively large magnitude for the longer-term series, support the interpretation that interest rate risk is the result of nonstationarity and increases with term to maturity. The absence of serial dependence in the longer-term series further supports the notion that interest rate risk results from disturbances to the system rather than from noise in a stationary system.

The survey evidence in Chapter 5 suggests that portfolio managers are often likely to hold divergent expectations and may well take speculative positions on the basis of them. The evidence on distributed lag forecasting models supports this interpretation indirectly because the simplest naive forecasting model does as well as the more elaborate ones: a forecast of no change in rates can hardly give rise to widespread divergence of expectations regarding the course of rates. Finally, the results reviewed in this chapter support the notion that considerations that cannot be comprehended by rational maximizing rules under stationary conditions govern nonspeculative portfolio policies and that risk aversion is a ubiquitous phenomenon.

There seems, then, to be considerable support for the notion that a policy to influence the level and structure of rates through altering the maturity composition of the outstanding federal debt should meet with success. Let us now turn to the question of debt management policy.

chapter 7

Debt Management Policy

The objectives of stabilization policy—full employment, price stability, economic growth and balanced international payments—can be reached by a variety of means. The tools of policy available to the stabilization authorities include open market operations, the discount rate, reserve requirements, taxation, government expenditures, and deficit financing not to mention a host of specialized measures applicable to particular institutions and markets. The management of the maturity composition of the federal debt is but one among these policy tools and not a more important one at that. It may nevertheless be an effective supplement to other tools in the execution of policy. We begin this final chapter with a brief consideration of the possible costs and benefits of maturity management as a stabilization tool. After this we will briefly review the debt management practices of the Federal Reserve and the Treasury, the two agencies which direct control of the maturity composition of the debt. We will then consider some of the evidence bearing on the responsiveness of the term structure to maturity composition. We will close with some general considerations for future policy.

A. POLICY ALTERNATIVES AND RECENT PRACTICE

Changes in the maturity composition of the government debt could help to achieve the goals of stabilization policy by helping to induce countercyclical changes in the level and structure of interest rates. One theoretical basis for this is the term premium hypothesis, though even the segmented market hypothesis predicts that shifts in relative supply of differing maturities will lead to corresponding shifts in yields to maturity.[1] Keeping to the line of rea-

---

[1] The reason for the twist effect under the term premium hypothesis is that the authorities alter the total amount of interest rate risk to be borne by the

146

soning already developed in this book, increases in the average maturity will cause all interest rates to rise because the total amount of interest rate risk to be borne is thereby increased, and all financial assets are subject to this risk. Other things equal, higher rates will reduce private investment expenditures and, consequently, would be a useful adjunct to a decline in the rate of growth of the money stock on a movement toward a full employment budget surplus. Similarly, a shortening of the debt would tend to lower the level of rates. During a recession, shortening would tend to increase private investment expenditures. In addition to altering the level of rates, changes in maturity could lead to changes in the structure, decrease in average maturity lowering long rates more than short and, some believe, even raising short rates. We shall return to the possibility of twisting the term structure shortly. For the moment, let us consider what costs such a debt management policy might entail.

Some critics of stabilization policy hold that the stabilization authorities are themselves a significant producer of instability in the economic system.[2] For them, management of the maturity composition is likely to introduce problems in its own right. For example, M. Friedman argues explicitly that the maturity composition should be established once and for all, and the debt rolled over on a regular basis so that no difficulty could arise from uncertainty surrounding maturity management policies [21, pp. 60ff]. Thus, under his proposal not only would the maturity of debt be excluded as a policy tool, but it would not be tailored to accommodate institutional preferences.

On the other side are those who believe that these dangers are exaggerated.[3] They espouse a judicious manipulation of debt maturity as part of an overall stabilization strategy. If such a policy is to be adopted, it would be helpful to know with sufficient precision how the private financial sector responds to alterations in maturity composition to permit quantitative specification of policy actions. As we shall see, the evidence available can provide little guidance of a quantitative kind. Before turning to the evidence it may be useful to review the recent maturity policies of the Federal Reserve and the

---

private sector. This change makes portfolio managers and private decision makers more or less cautious in the pursuit of their own policy objectives. Under the segmented market hypothesis the change in the structure of rates reflects shifts in relative supply but does not affect behavior of portfolio managers nor, presumably other private decision makers, since all are locked into their present behavior by institutional habits.

[2] See, for example, M. Friedman [21], and K. Brunner and A. H. Meltzer [6].

[3] See, for example, A. Okun [52].

Treasury. In the absence of vigorous maturity management actions, it is unlikely that much can be learned about impact of changes in maturity composition.

In the early sixties the Federal Reserve adopted a policy of being prepared to buy and sell securities of long as well as short maturities after nearly a decade of explicit avoidance of open market transactions in long-term debt. The Federal Reserve has from time to time advanced rationales for its maturity policies, though these have seemed designed to justify policy after the fact more than to guide its formulation. The formulation of monetary policy is too complex and important a story to be told in the space available here.[4]   Instead, we shall confine our attention to the shift from a policy of conducting open market operations in short-term securities, the "bills only" policy to one in which transactions in all maturities become permissible.

The shift away from "bills only" occurred in the early years of the Kennedy Administration. When the new administration took office, the economy was very nearly at the trough of the 1960–61 recession. Unemployment had not only reached a disturbingly high level; it had remained above "normal" during the recovery from the previous recession of 1958. Persistent balance of payment deficits had accompanied the recovery and the subsequent recession and in even 1960 and 1961 large outflows of short-term capital occurred. The new administration and the monetary authorities were under considerable pressure to attack on both fronts, thereby inducing a rapid recovery and expansion of employment and reducing or reversing short-term capital outflows. A major response to this pressure was "Operation Twist," an attempt to lower long-term rates and simultaneously raise short-term rates, which is to say, to twist the term structure, by shortening the average maturity of marketable government debt in the hands of the public.

Whether twisting, if successful, would contribute significantly to recovery and reduction of balance of payment deficits is an important question but one which we cannot pursue here. The question of primary significance to us at this point is whether the Federal Reserve succeeded in their attempt to twist the term structure, and if not, what changes in maturity composition would be required to achieve it. The record of open market operations during the years 1961-64—after this period unemployment was no longer a major problem—reveal a cautious pursuit of Operation Twist.[5]   Open

---

[4] See Intext series on Monetary Theory and Policy [47, 71].

[5] The Federal Reserve efforts in this direction were compared with "the caution of a nun undertaking the study of comparative theology [38, p. 233]."

market purchases of securities maturing after five years as a percentage of net outright purchases amount to 45.3 percent in 1961, 20.6 percent in 1962, 19.6 percent in 1963 and 18.9 percent in 1964.[6] However, at this same time, the average maturity in the hands of the public increased because of Treasury funding operations. Thus, while on December 31, 1960, securities due after five years were 24.26 percent of the debt outstanding, by December 31, 1964, securities in this maturity range had increased to 30.57 percent of the total [38, p. 235].

How can Treasury actions be reconciled with contrary actions of the Federal Reserve? In part, the answer must be that the Treasury was not a party to Operation Twist; the two agencies need not, and often do not, coordinate their efforts. Moreover, the Treasury has been committed to a policy of "tailoring" the debt to the market. This policy has two aspects of special concern to us.[7] First, it has meant selling long-term debt when rates are low during recessions and selling short-term debt when rates are high during booms, ostensibly to keep down the interest cost of the debt. This is precisely what happened in 1961 and 1962 when the Federal Reserve was buying long-term securities.

The other aspect of Treasury policy of concern, and, more properly, the tailoring aspect, is reflected in the way in which new issues reach the market. The Treasury consults with lending institutions, considering the "maturity" needs of a wide range of institutional holders. The consequence is usually a variety of issues with differing maturities with coupons slightly above the corresponding market yields to maturity.[8] Since 1965, the ceiling on long-term bonds has precluded this practice for securities over five years in maturity. In 1968, the issuance of seven-year notes provided the Treasury some leeway around the coupon ceiling. As noted in Chapter 6, the average maturity of the outstanding debt peaked in 1965. Until 1968, when the seven-year notes came into existence, the passage of time shortened the average maturity in the absence of new long-term issues. Thus, while there have been changes in maturity composition

[6] Net outright purchases are total purchases of securities in the open market less sales and redemptions. In 1961 these amounted to $788 million out of a total of $153 billion total outstanding in the hands of the public. Of this latter amount, $37 billion matured in over five years [38, pp. 234–235].

[7] We focus on interest minimization and tailoring because the preceding analysis bears most directly on these aspects of policy, especially the latter. For a fuller discussion of Treasury policy see such works as Gaines [24], Smith [61], and Friedman [21].

[8] By offering to exchange new securities of longer maturity having relatively high coupons for outstanding securities with lower coupons and shorter maturities, the Treasury reduces the reluctance of portfolio managers to trade in longer-term issues.

of the marketable government debt, they have been at best moderate in magnitude and not the consequence of a concerted effort to use maturity composition to achieve stabilization objectives. Indeed, these changes may reflect a policy of accommodating shifts in demand. Let us now turn to the studies that have attempted to measure the impact of these rather moderate changes in maturity composition on the term structure.

B. TESTING THE EFFECTS OF CHANGING THE MATURITY COMPOSITION

According to the term premium hypothesis, altering maturity composition affects security prices, given the other underlying variables determining interest rates, because it changes the volume of interest rate risk that must be borne. This total volume depends on characteristics of nongovernmental financial assets and under conditions of uncertainty, ultimately on durability and immobility of the real assets which lie behind the financial ones. Over time the interest rate risk associated with private financial and real assets can change. To estimate the impact of changes in public debt requires that changes in the characteristics of private financial assets be taken into account. The data on private financial assets is not adequate to permit reasonable statistical control of such changes in regression analyses.[9] In such analyses no attempt is made to account for changes in the characteristics of private financial assets.

Moreover, classifying the maturities of government debt for inclusion in regression analyses is not easy unless there is to be a separate maturity for each issue. However, a reasonable division of the outstanding debt into a few categories of maturity is possible.[10] A much more difficult problem is that of dealing with call features. Indeed, the call appears to owe its existence to the possibility of divergent views about the course of rates. If yields to maturity fall below coupon rates, market price will rise above par, but of course not above the call price. If the issuer obtained a relatively favorable call price, he could refund the issue with lower coupons when rates fell. On the other hand, the initial buyer may have paid a price sufficiently low to compensate him for this possibility. If buyers and sellers agreed on the likely course of rates, the call price and purchase price would be so adjusted as to make it a matter of indifference whether there was a call feature or not. If buyers and sellers had

---

[9] For a discussion of the inadequacy of the data on private debt see Malkiel [38, p. 222].

[10] See Malkiel [38, p. 224].

divergent expectations, the call feature affords an opportunity for speculative gain one or the other side of the market.[11] In view of this, it is far from clear how to classify securities with call features. This issue is chiefly of interest, not because of the fuzziness it introduces into maturity categories owing to the practices of issuing government bonds with call features, but as evidence of the possibility of divergent expectations. As we shall see, the models used to estimate the impact of maturity composition implicitly assume homogeneous expectations.

Further, as the discussion of "tailoring" suggested, changes in maturity composition may stem from the desires of institutional lenders (demand) or from structure of rates itself, (Treasury supply) as with the efforts to minimize the interest burden of the debt. Consequently, empirical examination that views changes in maturity composition as causing changes in the term structure may be inappropriate. If the influence has chiefly run the other way, from the structure of yields to maturity composition, policy prescriptions based on regression analyses of the kind described below could, if followed, lead to consequences very different from those anticipated. We shall return to this point later.

One approach to measuring the impact of changes in the maturity composition of government debt on the term structure is that used by A. Okun [52] and by R. Scott [58]. They estimated a linear regression equation of the following kind:

$$(7\text{-}1) \qquad R_{L,t} - R_{S,t} = b_0 + b_1 D_T + b_2 A_T + b_3 Z$$

where the dependent variable is the spread between selected long and short yields to maturity, D_T is the total debt outstanding, A_T is an index of maturity and Z is a vector of macroeconomic variables. Okun used quarterly data from the 1946–1959 period and Scott used monthly data from the 1952–1959 period: thus, neither observed the effects of Operation Twist.[12]

Okun found the coefficients to suggest the hypothesis that changes in maturity composition influence the term structure. An

---

[11] Suppose the issues of a consol expected rates to fall whereas lenders expected rates to rise. Let the present purchase price be $1,000 for an annual payment of $40. If the interest rate declines from 4 percent to 3 percent, the price of a consol, in the absence of a call price would rise to $1,333. Lenders expecting rates to rise might accept a call price of, say, $1,200 at a purchase price of $1,000 because they do not expect the call option to be exercised. If they did, they would require some discount at purchase.

[12] This does not matter much since the maturity composition did not change much and did not shorten during the early sixties as we have seen. A further difficulty is that these two investigators defined some of their key variables differently which reduces the comparability of their results.

increase in average maturity would raise the long-term rate relative to the short-term rate but the effect would be slight. He estimated that the replacement of $1 billion of bills by $1 billion of 20-year bonds would increase the spread between long- and short-term rates by about three basis points. However, Scott found that a lengthening of the debt reduced the long-term rate by more than it decreased the short-term rate so that, as a consequence, the spread between long and short rates narrowed rather than widened with a lengthening of the debt. This is a very puzzling result. However, in light of the un- resolved difficulties just described it should not be surprising.

Perhaps the most troubling aspect of this approach is its inability or, at least, its failure to deal explicitly with the influence of expecta- tional variables on the term structure. J. Wood sought to separate explicitly the effects of changes in expectation from those produced by changes in maturity composition [70]. However, like Okun and Scott, he treated changes in maturity as independent of changes in the term structure, in effect, like them, begging the question of the determinants of debt management policy. Wood used first dif- ferences rather level of the main regression variables to eliminate the auto correlation in the residuals.[13] He found that most coefficients relating to changes in maturity composition were not significantly different from zero. The conclusions that probably should be drawn from this are (1) time series regression relating levels of the spread between long and short rates to level of maturity composition and related variables can be misleading because of strong time trends in all variables, and (2) in the absence of pronounced autonomous debt management actions it is very difficult to judge what impact an aggressive policy would have.

N. Wallace took yet a different approach to estimating the influence of maturity composition [67]. To test whether changes in maturity composition influence the term structure, he developed the hypothesis that forward one-period rates would reflect the brunt of the effect of exogenous changes in the supply of the corresponding forward one-period loans. What is novel here is Wallace's treatment of bonds as a succession of one-period forward loans. Thus, a five year bond may be regarded as a succession of one year renewable loans, the first one being current and the remaining four being forward loans. He then regressed a measure of forward rates on an index of the relative supply of the applicable forward loans as follows:

---

[13] It is not clear in the cases of Okun and Scott whether auto correlation, which could have affected their interpretation of the findings, existed.

$$(7\text{-}2) \qquad \log \left[\frac{1 + r_{1,t,t+n}}{1 + R_{1,t}} \right] = a + b_n \left[\frac{M_{t,t+n+1}}{M_{t,t+n}} \right]$$

where $r_{1,t,t+n}$ is the currently observed forward rate applicable to period $t + n$, $R_{1,t}$ is the current one-period rate, $M_{t,t+n+1}$ is the quantity of the outstanding debt maturity at or after the end of period $t + n$ and hence which contains forward loans applicable to period $t + n$, and $M_{t,t+n}$ is the quantity of debt not containing such forward loans.

Using quarterly data for the period 1946 through 1962, Wallace found a positive but weak association between the maturity composition variable and the dependent which he interpreted as supporting the view that risk aversion requires yield differentials to induce holders to lengthen the maturity of their holdings. At the same time, these finds are subject to the qualifications already noted. In particular, there is nothing in Wallace's procedure that takes account of the possibility that changes in the independent variables are not actually exogenous because of tailoring of the debt.

Terrell and Frazer present some evidence on the maturity composition effect which they regard as supporting the view that changes in maturity composition are primarily endogenous, reflecting the commitment of Treasury to a tailoring policy [64, p. 31]. In this respect, their work differs fundamentally from that just reviewed, although the equation they estimate resembles the ones other investigators have used. It is as follows:

$$(7\text{-}3) \qquad \log \frac{R_S}{R_L} = a + b \log \frac{V_s}{V_L}$$

where R_S is the 90-day bill rate, R_L, yield to maturity on government bonds maturing in ten or more years, V_s, the quantity of marketable debt maturing in less than five years, and V_L, the quantity of marketable debt maturing in more than five years. They posit that, because change in maturity composition largely reflects the preferences of lenders, the relationship should be a very weak one, and if anything, negative. The reason for this is that shifts in maturity undertaken by the Treasury would reflect accommodation to demand pressure. Consequently, such shifts would be accompanied by, if anything, an increase in price (decline in yield) on the maturities that were in demand. Thus, in Eq. 7-3, if V_L increases because of demand considerations, R_L would not change or would decrease, with the result that the coefficient b would be negative.

They fitted monthly data to Eq. 7-3 for eight overlapping two year periods, beginning with July 1960–June 1962 and ending with July 1967–June 1969.[14]   Six of the eight regression coefficients are negative, and the two which are positive—those for the July 1966–June 1968 and the July 1967–June 1969 subperiods—are not significantly different from zero.   Two of the negative coefficients—those for the July 1961–June 1963 and July 1964–June 1966 subperiods—are significantly negative at the 1 percent level of significance.[15]   This study does not control for variations in the maturity composition of private debt nor does it deal with the other difficulties described above facing such effects.   Its principal virtue is that it explicitly recognizes that maturity management of the government debt has been aimed chiefly at accommodating lending institutions.[16] The definitive study on the impact of changes in maturity composition remains to be done.

Even though the average maturity of the government debt increased during the period following the Federal Reserve's announced intention to twist the term structure, the announcement itself may have had an impact quite apart from changes in maturity it might have had.   Malkiel notes that from December 31, 1960 to December 31, 1964, bill yields rose 147 basis points while bond yields rose only 23 basis points [38, p. 237].   He goes on to say that "[i]t would appear . . . that the monetary authorities were successful in engineering a substantial increase in short rates while restraining the rise in long rates."   While Malkiel emphasizes the tentativeness of this inference, he goes on to suggest that announcement of the change policy could have led market participants to alter their views on what the "normal" range of interest rates was causing the change in the term structure just noted.   In terms of the distributed lag forecasting models discussed in Chapter 5, one version of which Malkiel uses, the public commitment of the Federal Reserve to conduct open market operations in long-term securities as well as short-term ones, could have altered the "expectations forming mechanism."

It is worth examining this line of reasoning in some detail for it highlights the major point of difference between the approach to forecasting as an ingredient in speculative behavior taken in this book and the distributed lag approach that characterizes most of the work in the field.   This difference has important implications for the conduct of debt management policy.   We will turn to these implications shortly.   Malkiel is suggesting that the parameters of the mech-

---

[14] The results are not affected if the overlaps are omitted. See [64].
[15] Modigliani and Sutch [50] get similar results.
[16] It also uses more recent data.

anism by which the market extrapolates from past to future interest rates can be altered by what the stabilization authorities say as much as by what they do.[17] The conclusions reached in Chapter 5, that the performance of extrapolative forecasting mechanisms are largely statistical artifacts, raises some question about how an announcement effect might work. If announcements cannot affect the parameters of nonexistent mechanisms, what do they affect?

To raise this question is to attempt to go behind the assertion that the market behaves "as if" expectations were found by an extrapolative mechanism of some kind. In the first place the evidence supporting this assertion is itself questionable as we have seen. However, even if the evidence did support the assertion, the policy issue remains as to how policy actions affect the management of institutional portfolios. It has been argued at some length that financial intermediaries provide services of fundamental importance in their effort to capture speculative gains. Without the collection and processing information on the underlying variables affecting the level and structure of rates involved in speculative behavior, interest rates could not serve as measures of opportunity cost. In terms of this conception of forecasting we may ask how announcements affect forecasting activity. And closely related is the question of how alterations of maturity composition would affect forecasting activity.

To speculate successfully, portfolio managers need information on a wide range of variables, including policy actions of the stabilization authorities. Forecasting stabilization variables can be divided into two parts; (1) forecasting policy posture; and (2) forecasting the events that will elicit policy actions given this posture. The interrelationship between these two forecasting activities is not simple, nor is either activity simple in itself.[18] Let us confine our attention here to some aspects of forecasting policy posture. It would appear that announced intentions would be an important ingredient in forecasting the course of policy actions. Changes in announced policy might well lead to changes in forecasts of the course of policy. However, policy posture and policy action are not identical.

Portfolio managers may well attend to what stabilization authori-

17 See Malkiel [38, p. 245] for a discussion of the announcement effect.
18 I do not mean to suggest that forecasting is so complex and difficult that it is not, as a practical matter, feasible. Staffs of financial intermediaries are employed on a continuous basis. There should be something of substantial difficulty involved, given the resources so consumed. What is required is that forecasters do sufficiently better than chance to cover the costs involved in forecasting. This clearly does not mean achieving perfection or even anticipating novelty. It does mean being alert to novelty and moving quickly on new information. The emphasis on the difficulty of forecasting seems appropriate in light of the oversimplications of the process generally to be found in the literature.

ties say as well as to what they do. But the passage of time affords
the opportunity for learning whether the authorities mean what they
say. Referring to Malkiel's inference just cited about the connection
between the intention to twist, the narrowing of the spread between
short and long-term rates, and the increase in the average maturity of
the debt over the period, the portfolio managers might well have concluded that the authorities did not mean what they said. Moreover,
maturity management is but one aspect of stabilization policy.[19]
Statements on other and more important aspects of stabilization
policy posture are often not free from ambiguity. What is of concern
to us here is impact of this ambiguity. The question of appropriate
policy should not be considered apart from the difficulty particular
policies introduce into the forecasting process because of the uncertainty entailed by the associated policy postures. We shall return to
this point shortly.

Turning now to the policy actions more directly, let us consider
what the impact on information collection and processing in an intermediary would be of an announced policy of changing maturity composition. For massive changes in maturity composition we have no direct evidence. Indeed, for any but minor changes we have no direct
evidence. However, given the character of speculative forecasting as
described here, large changes in maturity composition over short periods could be very disruptive for portfolio managers who have relatively inflexible information processing systems. The Treasury's
policy of tailoring the debt has permitted financial intermediaries to
adapt more slowly than otherwise to changing conditions in the
private and public liability and asset markets.

In an environment in which the Treasury and Federal Reserve
followed a coordinated policy of sharp and sizable shifts in maturity
compositions of the government debt, financial intermediaries might
well have developed portfolio management systems capable of more
flexible responses than they now can make. To achieve this flexibility would entail costs. It would be difficult to spell out what would
be involved. The academic literature is not of much help, especially
that reviewed here, since in it portfolio management in a nonstationary context is not seen as a central problem. A thorough going analysis of this problem would require a separate study.[20] At the very
least, flexibility may be presumed to reduce the opportunity for
specialization among financial intermediaries. Thus, there might be,

[19] See Malkiel [38, p. 225] for a discussion which recognizes the difficulties
of specifying a supply function of the government debt.
[20] Such a study should include observation of institutional portfolio management going a good deal beyond survey methods.

in addition to the cost of transition, increments in current operating costs necessary for a larger, less specialized information processing systems. Whatever a proper study of this question would uncover, it is clear that the distributed lag approach to forecasting obscures the need to consider the impact of what the stabilization authorities say and do on the forecasting activities of portfolio managers.

C. RECOMMENDATIONS FOR DEBT MANAGEMENT POLICY

In the light of these considerations and of the evidence reviewed and the analysis advanced in this book, what is the best policy for the stabilization authorities to adopt? Beyond the stricture that the Federal Reserve and the Treasury should not act at cross purposes, there appear to be three main alternatives. The authorities can alter the maturity composition of the government debt in coordination with other policy variables to achieve broad stabilization objectives. They can establish a relatively fixed maturity composition schedule together with a set of procedures to govern the issuance and retirement of debt that effectively eliminate maturity composition as a tool of stabilization policy. Finally, the Treasury can continue to tailor the debt to the market in a coordinated effort to reduce the uncertainty caused by policy posture and policy actions, thereby facilitating the information processing function of the private financial sector. Broad stabilization strategies would employ other policy tools. Let us consider each of these alternatives in somewhat more detail.

There is no precedent for making debt management part of an overall stabilization strategy. As we have seen, Operation Twist was chiefly a posture taken by the Federal Reserve that facilitated a move away from the earlier "bills only" policy. The Treasury was not committed to it. The fact is that the authorities have never undertaken major alterations in the maturity composition of the government debt of a magnitude likely to produce measurable effects on policy targets such as the levels of economic activity, employment and international money flows. Thus, the authorities do not know how to achieve the desired effects on policy targets. Nor do they know what side effects such massive shifts might produce in the private financial sector.

Following the line of reasoning developed just above, the side effects would not be negligible. Such a policy would be tantamount to antitailoring: rather than simplifying the forecasting and management problems of portfolio managers, it would complicate them. It may be, of course, that after financial intermediaries had had an opportunity to develop more flexible systems of portfolio management, a policy of massive intervention in maturity composition could be accommodated by the private financial sector with relative ease. Whether such a result would finally obtain is an open question. Unfortunately, not only do we not know the answer, but the question itself hardly seems to be understood. Perhaps the greatest shortcomings of the comparative static framework, with the hedging pressure motives of interest rate risk and distributed lag forecasting models which accompany it, within which analysis of these issues have largely been conducted, is that it prevents this kind of question from being asked. In view of the considerable ignorance about both the principal and side effects of a policy of massive intervention, the best that can be said for it is that it should not be considered for adoption until reasonably satisfactory answers to the relevant questions have been obtained.

The second alternative is one of neutralizing debt management. Not only are efforts to minimize the interest cost of the debt by procyclical issuance of long-term debt during troughs and short-term debt at peaks in economic activity ruled out, but any attempts to manipulate maturity composition to accommodate the market are ruled out as well. The principal arguments advanced to support this policy are two. One is that tailoring is best done by the market; that is, financial intermediaries can convert the maturity composition of the government by issuing liabilities of whatever maturity is desired more readily than the Treasury can. The second is that the present policy of tailoring "is a fertile source of confusion, uncertainty and instability" [22, p. 63]. Let us consider these arguments a little more fully.

To treat financial intermediaries as repackaging agencies, converting government debt of given maturities into debt of their own or with maturities more suitable to the market is to ignore them as active agencies with their own utility functions and to gloss over the essential characteristics of interest rate risk. According to institutional utility function hypothesis, what intermediaries package for the market is not liabilities but rather their own common stock which, as a result of the risk and yield characteristics of their assets and liabilities taken together, serves as a diversified portfolio with given risk and yield characteristics and is understood as such by the market. The risk characteristics are to be understood, not in the static equilibrium context but in a nonstationary one so that a significant element in the market's understanding of the institution is the amount of interest rate risk associated with its common stock. Assuming that financial intermediaries play an active role of this kind, what would the consequence be if, to accommodate the market as this second alternative would require, the intermediary acquired long-term government debt, thereby lengthening the average maturity of its asset portfolio, and omitted very short-term liabilities correspondingly shortening the average maturity of liabilities.

Given that interest rate risk depends on the span of time covered rather than hedging pressures, an increase in the average maturity of assets will increase the interest rate risk associated with the intermediary's common stock. Similarly a reduction in the average maturity of the liabilities shifts interest rate risk from the intermediary's creditors to its stockholders. Taking the opposite case, the conversion of short-term government debt into longer-term institutional liabilities, the interest rate risk associated with the intermediary's equity would decline because of the decline in risk or the assets and the liabilities. Thus, tailoring by the market—that is, by intermediaries rather than the Treasury, causes the intermediary to change, as it were, its institutional utility function which is to say, to change the risk and return characteristics of its common equity. Changes of this kind entail costs which cannot be easily incorporated in the usual comparative static analysis and so tend to be ignored. Recognizing the role financial intermediaries play in the collection and processing of information in the nonstationary context, changes of the kind entailed by institutional "tailoring," would increase the management problems these institutions face. Not only must they maintain an information processing capacity but they must make clear to the market their policy objectives and what these imply for the characteristics of their common stock. The evidence reviewed in Chapter 6 suggests that one way to help the market gain this understanding is to maintain a fairly stable overall portfolio policy on an industry-wide basis. If they abandon this stability, they must find some alternative way to create this understanding.[21] It is likely that the present policy of maintaining fairly stable policy objectives is the least costly way to do this. Furthermore, ignoring this cost, holders of such stock might find themselves in the position of either accepting frequent shifts in the risk characteristics of their portfolio or engaging in frequent transactions to keep the level of risk they bear relatively steady.

If the maturity composition of the debt becomes stable (more

[21] It is not clear what such an alternative would be. The market's understanding of the objectives of financial institutions and the characteristics of their common stock is not the result of an explicit public relations effort but rather the consequence of an accumulation of observation and experience of institutional behavior. Because of its "found" (not made) character, it is very difficult to devise ways to manipulate this understanding.

stable than under present policy) under a policy of neutral management it might appear that the need for intermediaries to tailor would be virtually eliminated. This would be true to the extent that a major source, if not the major source of nonstationarity was a stabilization policy itself. If significant disturbances arise outside the government sector, then the stability of maturity composition provided by neutral debt management could be dysfunctional since it would preclude the possibility of Treasury action to assist intermediaries in their efforts to cope with such disturbances. This brings us to the second point proponents of neutral management have made; namely, that the Treasury, through its efforts to tailor the debt, is a source of "confusion, uncertainty, and instability."

It may well be that in the execution of stabilization policy the authorities became a significant source of disruption. But, as has already been noted, debt management is but one of the tools available to the authorities in their pursuit of the goals of stabilization policy. For example, open market operations, whether in bills only or not, have in the view of some writers, been procyclical rather than stabilizing.[22] What is not clear is that the Treasury's tailoring efforts have produced similar destabilization consequences. At issue here is the relative importance of the sources of nonstationarity in the system and it is an issue about which there is considerable disagreement. Those who advance neutral debt management believe that shifts in the nonpolicy variables that determine the course of interest rates—productivity, thrift, population, tables technology, and the like—would pose no serious portfolio management problems. Others believe the stabilizing authorities have a vital role to play in helping the private financial sector cope with the disturbances which arise in the private sector. This latter possibility brings us to the third alternative of continuing the present policy.

Recent debt management policy, as we have seen, has been a combination of tailoring, attempts to reduce the interest burden of the debt and, early in the decade of the 60's, minor, even miniscule, attempts to twist the term structure. A debt management policy centered primarily in tailoring seems the most consistent with the character of instability or nonstationarity of the system proposed here as the fundamental source of interest rate risk. Arguments against massive intervention in maturity composition have already been considered. We know so little about the effects of such a policy that efforts to follow it might well make the system more unstable. As for reducing the interest burden of the debt, we have already noted that a succession of varying short-term yields might produce a

[22] For example, see Brunner and Meltzer [6].

higher average interest charge than is readily apparent from observing yields to maturity at a given period in time. Thus, selling short-term issues at peaks could partly offset reductions in interest costs obtained by selling long-term issues at troughs.[23] There are other factors which complicate the relationships between the interest burden and maturity composition and thereby call into question burden minimization as a policy objective. A full analysis of these complications is beyond the scope of this book, so that we will not pursue the matter further here.[24] Let us turn, then, to the issues involved in the tailoring policy.

The thrust of the evidence and argument of the previous chapters has been that the environment portfolio managers face is not a steady state one in which risk is primarily actuarial, but rather one of non-stationarity in which management is an ongoing and never ending process. What is at issue here is the relative weight of the private and public sectors as sources of instability. In my view, policy actions are much too infrequent to be the major source of difficulty.[25]

The theory of private sector instability suggested in Chapter 3 was a rather eclectic one; namely, that in a large, complex system, disturbances can arise from a multiplicity of sources so that, in the absence of the possibility of complete knowledge of the system, disturbances cannot be regarded as arising out of some higher level stationary process. If we cannot estimate the parameters of such a process, we cannot distinguish between the possibility that we know nothing about them and the possibility that they do not exist. It may help to place this theory in perspective if we consider a less eclectic theory of private sector instability, also capable of providing a basis for a tailoring policy and which stands over against the notion that the stabilization authorities are the principal source of instability.

H. Minsky has argued that the "fundamental issue in monetary theory is whether a capitalist economy is inherently stable or whether, due to its very nature, it is unavoidably unstable" [48, p. 223]. In his view,

> capitalism is inherently flawed, being prone to booms, crises and depressions. This instability . . . is due to characteristics the financial system must possess if it is to be consistent with full blown capitalism.

[23] Recall that, as shown in Chapter 4, an extrapolating portfolio manager with short-term assets would have realized a higher yield over the period than one with short-term assets. The inverse of this is that an extrapolating borrower, say the Treasury, would have done better to emit long-term debt.

[24] See Friedman [21, p. 62] for a discussion of the impact of interest minimization on the money supply. See also Laidler [35] and De Prano [15].

[25] The standard deviation of the time series of Treasury bond-holding period yields shows that relatively large price movements are quite frequent, much more frequent than major policy actions.

> Such a financial system will be capable of both generating signals that
> induce an accelerating desire to invest and of financing that accelerating
> investment. [48, p. 224]

Two points are of particular interest here; (1) the required characteristics of the financial system, and (2) the mechanisms by which the
signals inducing instability arise.

According to Minsky, capitalism requires "indirect and layered
ownership"; which is to say, financial intermediaries. These institutions, together with "the existence of a wide array of permissible
liability structures and a large menu of financial assets," facilitate
"the changing of portfolios and the adjustment of liability structures." He goes on to assert that

> Before the impact and efficacy of money can be traced it is necessary
> to specify the financial institutions; monetary economics cannot escape
> being institutional economics. Once the problem of monetary theory is
> identified as revolving around the financing of positions in the stock of
> assets and the financing of additions to the stock, then a portfolio or
> asset-management view of the monetary process is natural. [48, p. 225]

Thus, Minsky gives a central place to asset management under uncertainty. However, he does not develop fully a model of portfolio
management such as the industry-wide utility function hypothesis,
though there is nothing in his analysis which precludes such an
explanation. Indeed, he very much wants to move away from "an
Elysian state of moving equilibrium" [48, p. 229].

His chief interest is, once the centrality of portfolio management
is established, to advance a theory of the behavior of expectations in
a capitalistic system. Minsky believes that "[e]xpectations and tastes
for uncertainty are affected by success and failure of the economy....
Although the effect of the past upon expectations may be considered
to be continuous, it is possible to interpret history as showing that
dramatic changes [discontinuities] in the taste for uncertainty have
occurred" [48, pp. 227-228]. Thus, portfolio managers can, by projecting recent trends, help produce booms. But more importantly,
managers can panic and by drastically revising their expectations
downward, can cause crises and even depressions. What is crucially
significant for Minsky is that, in a capitalist system, the authorities
cannot directly control these central aspects of private portfolio
management. They must, perforce, rely on indirect means of coping
with the ramifications of portfolio management under uncertainty.

Minsky is concerned with the question of discretion versus rules
over the broad range of stabilization policy. We shall confine our
attention to the conduct of debt management policy. Accommodation of the preferences of portfolio managers for particular assets ma-

turity affords the Treasury a means to reduce the complexity of portfolio management.   In particular, managers can be freed from concerns about changing the characteristics of their equality and focus their time and energy to the collection and processing of information. To the extent that tailoring permits and enhances this focusing of resources, the market will become more efficient; that is, more resources will be available for the kind of speculative activity which brings information on the underlying variables to bear as a significant influence on market prices. The easier it is for stabilizing speculation of this kind to be undertaken, presumably the more difficult it is for destabilizing speculation of the kind Minsky described to take hold.

This last statement should be qualified in some way since no evidence has been adduced here to support it. However, not much evidence is available. A major reason why we have not explored in substantive detail forecasting activity as it relates to stabilizing speculation is that the analytical framework typically used provides little room, for it has not been thought important to do so. The reasons for this state of affairs are many, but a major one is that we can get answers to questions only if the questions are asked and, by and large, the right questions have not been asked in this area.

However, if this line of reasoning is not too far from the mark, inquiry into the substance the portfolio management in financial intermediaries should provide an opportunity to determine the extent to which tailoring by the Treasury, and coordination of open market operations with Treasury actions, serves to increase the efficiency of the government bond market.[26]

[26] All large corporations are to some extent financial intermediaries in that they diversify their asset holdings. Inquiry should not be limited to financial intermediaries commonly recognized as such.

References

1. Stephen H. Archer and Charles A. D'Ambrosio (eds.), *The Theory of Business Finance: A Book of Readings* (New York: Macmillan, 1967).

2. Martin J. Bailey, "Discussion," *American Economic Review*, 54 (May 1964), 554.

3. William J. Baumol, *Economic Theory and Operations Analysis*, 3d ed. (Englewood Cliffs, N. J.: Prentice-Hall, 1972).

4. Frank J. Bonello, *The Formulation of Expected Interest Rates* (East Lansing, Mich.: Bureau of Business and Economics Research, Michigan State University, 1969).

5. Dawson E. Brewer and Jacob B. Michaelsen, "The Cost of Capital, Corporation Financing and the Theory of Investment Comment," *American Economic Review* 55 (June 1965), 516–524.

6. Karl Brunner and Allan H. Meltzer, *The Federal Reserve's Attachment to the Free Reserve Concept* (Washington: House Committee on Banking and Currency, 1964).

7. _____ , "The Uses of Money: Money in the Theory of an Exchange Economy," *The American Economic Review* 61 (December 1971), 784–805.

8. A. Buse, "Interest Rates, The Meiselman Model and Random Numbers," *The Journal of Political Economy* 75 (February 1967), 49–62.

9. Deane Carson and Ira O. Scott, Jr., "Commercial Book Attributes and Attitudes to Risk," *Banking and Monetary Studies*, edited by Deane Carson (Homewood, Ill.: Richard D. Irwin, 1963), 420–436.

10. Samuel B. Chase, Jr., "The Lock-in Effect: Bank Reactions to Securities Losses," *Monthly Review* (Federal Reserve Bank of Kansas City, June 1960), 9–16.

11. Kalman J. Cohen and Richard M. Cyert, *Theory of the Firm:*

Resource Allocation in a Market Economy (Englewood Cliffs, N. J.: Prentice-Hall, 1965).

12. Joseph W. Conard, *An Introduction to the Theory of Interest* (Berkeley, Calif.: University of California Press, 1963).

13. J. M. Culbertson, "The Term Structure of Interest Rates," *Quarterly Journal of Economics* 71 (November 1957), 485-517.

14. Frank DeLeeuw, "A Model of Financial Behavior," *The Brookings Quarterly Economic Model of the United States*, edited by J. S. Duerenberry, et al. (Chicago: Rand McNally, 1965), 465-530.

15. M. Deprano, *Money, Money Supply, and Money Control* (Scranton, Pa.: Intext Educational Publishers, forthcoming).

16. Stanley Diller, "Extrapolations, Anticipations and the Term Structure of Interest Rates" (Ph. D. dissertation, Columbia University, 1966).

17. David Durand, *Basic Yields of Corporate Bonds, 1900-1942* (New York: National Bureau of Economic Research, Technical Paper No. 3, 1942).

18. _____ , "The Cost of Capital, Corporation Finance, and the Theory of Investment: Comment," *American Economic Review* 49 (September 1959), 639-655.

19. Eugene F. Fama, "Efficient Capital Markets: A Review of Theory and Empirical Work," *Journal of Finance* 25 (May 1970), 383-417.

20. Donald E. Farrar, *The Investment Decision Under Uncertainty* (Englewood Cliffs, N. J.: Prentice-Hall, 1962).

21. Milton Friedman, *A Program for Monetary Stability* (New York: Fordham University Press, 1959).

22. _____ , *The Optimum Quantity of Money and Other Essays* (Chicago: Aldine-Atherton, 1969).

23. William C. Freund and Edward D. Zinbarg, "Application of Flow of Funds to Interest-Rate Forecasting," *Journal of Finance* 18 (May 1963) 231-248.

24. Tilford C. Gaines, *Techniques of Treasury Debt Management* (New York: Free Press of Glencoe, 1962).

25. J. A. G. Grant, "Meiselman on the Structure of Interest Rates: A British Test," *Economica* 31 (February 1964), 51-71.

26. Myron A. Grove, "Models of the Maturity Profile of the Balance Sheet" (Ph. D. dissertation, Northwestern University, 1964).

27. W. B. Hickman, *The Term Structure of Interest Rates: An Exploratory Analysis* (New York: National Bureau of Economic Research, 1943), manuscript.

28. J. R. Hicks, *Value and Capital*, 2d ed. (London: Oxford Press, 1946).

29. Sidney Homer, et al., *Supply and Demand for Credit in 1971* (New York: Salomon Brothers, 1970).

30. Lawrence D. Jones, *Investment Policies of Life Insurance Companies* (Boston: Division of Research, Howard Business School, 1968).

31. Edward J. Kane and Burton G. Malkiel, "The Term Structure of Interest Rates: An Analysis of a Survey of Interest-Rate Expectations," *Review of Economics and Statistics* 69 (August 1967), 343–355.

32. Rueben A. Kessel, *The Cyclical Behavior of the Term Structure of Interest Rates* (New York: National Bureau of Economic Research, Occasional Paper 91, 1965).

33. J. M. Keynes, *The General Theory of Employment Interest and Money* (New York: Harcourt Brace Jovanovich, 1936).

34. Frank H. Knight, *Risk, Uncertainty and Profit* (New York: Harper & Row, Torchbook edition, 1965).

35. David E. W. Laidler, *The Demand For Money: Theories and Evidence* (Scranton, Pa.: Intext Educational Publishers, 1969).

36. Friedrich A. Lutz, "The Structure of Interest Rates," *Quarterly Journal of Economics* 55 (November 1940), 36–63.

37. Frederick R. Macaulay, *The Movements of Interest Rates, Bond Yields, and Stock Prices in the United States Since 1856* (New York: National Bureau of Economic Research, 1938).

38. Burton G. Malkiel, *The Term Structure of Interest Rates: Expectations and Behavior Patterns* (Princeton: Princeton University Press, 1966).

39. _____ , *The Term Structure of Interest Rates: Theory, Empirical Evidence* (New York: McCaleb-Seiler, 1970).

40. Benoit Mandelbrot, "New Methods in Statistical Economics," *Journal of Political Economy* 71 (October 1963), 421–440.

41. Harry Markowitz, *Portfolio Selection: Efficient Diversification of Investments* (New York: John Wiley and Sons Inc., 1959).

42. A. James Meigs, *Free Reserves and the Money Supply* (Chicago: University of Chicago Press, 1962).

43. David Meiselman, *The Term Structure of Interest Rates* (Englewood Cliffs, New Jersey: Prentice-Hall, 1962).

44. J. B. Michaelsen, "The Term Structure of Interest Rates: Comment," *Quarterly Journal of Economics*, 77 (February 1963), 166–174.

45. _____ , "The Term Structure of Interest Rates and Holding Period Yields on Government Securities," *Journal of Finance*, 20 (September 1965), 444–463.

46. _____ and Robert C. Goshay, "Portfolio Selection in Finan-

cial Intermediaries," *Journal of Financial and Quantitative Analysis*, 2 (June 1967), 166–199.

47. Norman Mintz, *International Monetary Relations* (Scranton, Pa: Intext Educational Publishers, forthcoming).

48. Hyman P. Minsky, "Private Sector Asset Management and the Effectiveness of Monetary Policy: Theory and Practice," *The Journal of Finance*, 24 (May 1969), 223–238.

49. Franco Modigliani and Merton H. Miller, "The Cost of Capital, Corporation Finance, and the Theory of Investments," *American Economic Review*, 48 (June 1958), 261–297.

50. _____ and Richard Sutch, "Innovations in Interest Rate Policy," *American Economic Review* 56 (May 1966), 178–197.

51. Stewart C. Myers, "A Time-State-Preference Model of Security Valuation," *Journal of Financial and Quantitative Analysis* 3 (March 1968), 1–34.

52. Arthur M. Okun, "Monetary Policy, Debt Management, and Interest Rates: A Quantitative Appraisal," in *Stabilization Policies* (Englewood Cliffs, N. J.: Prentice-Hall, 1963), 331–380.

53. Murray E. Polakoff, "Reluctance Elasticity, Least Cost, and Member-Bank Borrowing: A Suggested Integration," *Journal of Finance* 15 (March 1960), 1–18.

54. Joan Robinson, "The Rate of Interest," *Econometrica* 19 (April 1951), 102.

55. Richard Roll, "Investment Diversification and Bond Maturity," *Journal of Finance* 26 (March 1971), 51–66.

56. _____ , *The Behavior of Interest Rates* (New York: Basic Books, 1970).

57. Robert Schlaifer, *Introduction to Statistics for Business Decisions* (New York: McGraw-Hill, 1961).

58. Robert H. Scott, "Liquidity and the Term Structure of Interest Rates," *Quarterly Journal of Economics* 79 (February 1965), 135–145.

59. William F. Sharpe, "Capital Asset Prices: A Theory of Market Equilibrium under Conditions of Risk," *Journal of Finance* 19 (September 1964), 425–442.

60. _____ , *Portfolio Theory and Capital Markets* (New York: McGraw-Hill, 1970).

61. Warren Smith, *Debt Management in the United States*, Study Paper 19 in *Study of Employment, Growth and Price Levels* (Washington: Joint Economic Committee, 1960).

62. Lester G. Telser, "A Critique of Some Recent Empirical Research on the Explanation of the Term Structure of Interest Rates,"

The Journal of Political Economy 75 (August 1967), Supplement, 546–561.

63. William T. Terrell, "The Term Structure of Interest Rates, Portfolio Theory, and the Role of Length to Maturity in Selecting United States Government Securities" (Ph. D. dissertation, Vanderbilt University, 1970).

64. ――― and William J. Frazer, Jr., "Interest Rates, Portfolio Behavior, and Marketable Government Securities," *Journal of Finance* 27 (March 1972), 1–36.

65. James Tobin, "Liquidity Preference as Behavior Toward Risk," *Review of Economic Studies* 25 (February 1958), 65–86.

66. James Van Horne, "Interest-Rate Risk and the Term Structure of Interest Rates," *Journal of Political Economy* 73 (August 1965), 344–351.

67. Neil Wallace, "The Term Structure of Interest Rates and the Maturing Composition of the Federal Debt" (Ph. D. dissertation, University of Chicago, 1964).

68. Oliver E. Williamson, *The Economics of Discretionary Behavior: Managerial Objectives in a Theory of the Firm* (Englewood Cliffs, N. J.: Prentice-Hall, 1964).

69. John H. Wood, "Expectations, Errors and the Term Structure of Interest Rates," *Journal of Political Economy* 71 (April 1963), 160–171.

70. ――― , "An Econometric Model of the Term Structure of Interest Rates," manuscript (cited in [38]).

71. Leland Yeager, *Monetary Theory and Policy* (Scranton, Pa.: Intext Educational Publishers, forthcoming).

Index